Capel Berrow

Deism not consistent with the religion of reason and nature

Capel Berrow

Deism not consistent with the religion of reason and nature

ISBN/EAN: 9783337718961

Printed in Europe, USA, Canada, Australia, Japan

Cover: Foto ©Lupo / pixelio.de

More available books at **www.hansebooks.com**

DEISM

NOT CONSISTENT WITH THE

RELIGION

OF

REASON AND NATURE.

By CAPEL BERROW, A. M.

———

LONDON:

PRINTED FOR J. DODSLEY, IN PALL-MALL,

M,DCC.LXXX.

TO HIS

ROYAL HIGHNESS

GEORGE,

PRINCE of WALES.

FIRST in defcent as your Royal Highnefs is from our moft gracious Sovereign, and his all amiable and illuftrious Confort, eminent for, among other their *truly* patriotic virtues, that exemplary life of piety, practical as well as devotional, which gives fuch an added luftre to the diadem encircling the brow of each; perfected too as *you* are, by means of a well-directed mode of education, in the theory of a Britifh conftitution, and practifed, from *principle*, in the *moral* precepts of that religion to which it is fo nearly *allied*---not to mention thofe your

affiduous

affiduous refearches in the *region of fcience*, with fuch acknowledged fuccefs too, as the *mathematician*, the *claffic*, the *connoiffeur* in *the Belles Lettres*, the *virtú*, acquifitions which ferve to give to the world fo confeffedly, in the *auguft prince*, the fenfible and accomplifhed GENTLEMAN, I will not doubt of your attachment at the fame time, with a zeal congenial with that which glows fo unremittingly in the breafts of your royal parents, to the caufe of Chriftianity, genuine, *uncorrupted* Chriftianity, the *peculiar glory* of Proteftant communities in general, the chief corner-ftone in Great Britain's moft happily conftructed eftablifhment in church and ftate in particular.

In order therefore to counteract the unwearied ENDEAVOURS of MODERN DEISTS to argue away the *neceffity*, and in confequence the *credibility* of a *revealed* religion, to invalidate the authenticity, and, of courfe, the *authority* of that repofitory of the *Gofpel difpenfation* the *facred pages*, and to repel, by the force of *reafon*, attempts inimical, as thofe are,

to

to the *civil* interefts of *every Chriſtian* ſtate, and daily encreaſing to an alarming degree in *ours*---I venture to requeſt *your patronage* and protection of a performance, the ſum and ſubſtance of *a familiar epiſtle to a friend*, penned *formerly* with that *all*-intereſting object in view, and now, with the utmoſt deference, laid at your Royal Highneſs's feet by

Your moſt devoted ſervant,

CAPEL BERROW.

D E I S M

NOT CONSISTENT WITH THE

R E L I G I O N

O F

REASON and NATURE.

D E A R S I R,

WHEN I had laſt the pleaſure of a converſation with you at your houſe, you was pleaſed, from your wonted zeal for the cauſe of deiſm, to put into my hands a treatiſe, intitled, *Deiſm fairly ſtated, and fully vindicated,* which, agreeably to your requeſt, I have peruſed with great attention, making thoſe remarks, as I went along, which I now ſend for your peruſal. And this I do the more readily, as they afford anſwers to a ſuppoſed *non-neceſſity,* and, in

B   conſequence,

confequence, the incredibility of a *revealed* religion. To the authenticity therefore, and, of courfe, the authority of that repofitory of the Gofpel difpenfation, *the facred pages*, I will, in order to
avoid trefpafling upon your time and patience, take upon me to
fhew how incompatible the *Deifts* principles are with the boafted defign of deifm, as ftated by its formidable patron and defen-
der, compared with that *promifed* plan of redemption a future *univerfal reftitution :* but to the purpofe and to proofs.

From the beginning of the performance there occurs nothing
worthy our notice, till the author comes to his *definition* of deifm,
which is as follows :

" Deifm, fays he, properly fpeaking fo called, whatever ill ufage
it may have met with, is no other than the religion effential to
man, the true original *Religion of Reafon and Nature :* fuch as
was believed and practifed by *Socrates* and thofe of old; who were
as great ornaments, and did as much honour to human nature, as
any Chriftian ever did."

In the true idea of the *religion of reafon and nature,* I under-
ftand to be implied an attention to all *extraordinary* intimations of
our duty, as well as to fuch as arife from the *ufual* exertions of
our reafoning faculties. So that it may and muft comprehend not
only the obfervance of fuch rules as Socrates and other philofophers
taught and practifed, but a regard likewife to precepts delivered by
a *divine* inftructor, furnifhed with the requifite *credentials* as *Heaven's ambaffador.* Wherefore if to deifm our author unites not a
diftinct belief of *revelation,* he fhould confider himfelf as poffibly
falling fhort of the *religion of reafon and nature ;* which teaches,
or I know not what is meant by the religion of reafon and nature,
that every precept or point of knowledge, delivered *mediately* or-
immediately

immediately to us by God, demands from us a diftinguifhed reverence—as a feparate fuperaded obligation on our confciences. It is, of courfe, incumbent therefore upon our deift, before he prefumes to affimilate the caufe of deifm to the *religion of reafon and nature*, to prove that in the former is included all that the latter recommends. Now, this I conceive to be a criterion of the propriety of the above comparifon which deifts are fcarce apprifed of. —And yet till they make both agree apparently *in rejecting revelation*, they cannot pretend to fay that deifm, and the *religion of reafon and nature*, are abfolutely one and the fame uniform fimilar rule of moral agency. That we may therefore put the point here in difpute upon a proper foot of inquiry, and fee how far deifm, in its *antichriftian* fcheme of moral independency, can be juftified on the principles of *natural reafon and religion* ; I will fuppofe you urging, as a rational foundation for our Deift's infidel perfuafions, the three following, perhaps, only material arguments to be produced in their behalf.

Firft, It is not probable that any light, information or inftruction touching the Deity, or our duty to him (which, our Deift fays, is, properly fpeaking, a revelation, p. 17.) fhould have been communicated to men by an immediate, particular, fpecial interpofition of the Deity for that purpofe ; nor

Secondly, Does it appear, that Jefus Chrift was really the inftrument employed by the Deity to convey any fuch revelation to the world, fuppofing it not improbable that God may have been inclined at times to afford us one ; nor,

Laftly, Does the authority of thofe fcriptures, which are faid to be a moft faithful repofitory of that fame revelation, come to us fo clear and unqueftionable in that point as might be expected ;

nor

nor are the writings themselves so well calculated, as they ought to be, to answer those purposes for which they are presumed to be intended.

If these most formidable obstructions to a general reception of Christianity, these standing stumbling blocks in the way of deists should haply at length be removed, though but even to *your* conviction, I shall rest myself contented with expecting, what will amply recompence my trouble (if there be any in this address) the pleasure of having happily prevailed over the two hasty prejudices of a valued friend, and restored *one* at least, from among the infatuated and unthinking *many*, to a rational and manly faith. I shall not however *multiply* reasonings on each particular branch of the enquiry, but satisfy myself chiefly in the use of one argument alone, when that one alone seems to me conclusive. " First then, it is not probable, says the Deist, that any " light, information or instruction touching the Deity, or our duty " to him, &c. should have been communicated to men by an im- " mediate, particular, and special interposition of the Deity for that " purpose."—And wherefore ? Why my reason, say you, in support of the assertion, informs me, that the connatural notices in my breast are so sufficiently declarative of the Deity, and of my duty to him, to myself and to all mankind, as to render any further instructions in my way to future happiness useless, which therefore could not have been intended me by my Creator.

Your reason ! alas, another man's reason, as *he* terms it, informs him that there is no God. And if the religion of reason and nature consists only in consulting what every man calls his own reason, atheism might as easily be resolved into the religion of nature by those who at any time espoused that particular persuasion, as you be justified in rejecting revelation, because your reason informs you that it is absolutely unnecessary.

But

But hold, fay you again, by my reafon I do not mean the fuggeſtions of whim, prejudice, and partiality—nor a pervefe and reprobate mind ; but (what points out to me the Deity, and my duty to him and to all mankind, and is therefore the *religion of reafon and nature)* an unbiaſſed attention to the nature and fitneſs of things, a law in which is comprehended the whole extent of my duty conſidered in every relation and circumſtance of life ; a law obligatory upon every individual, and claimant of my attention therefore in preference to, and even independent of all other *fupernatural* guides to my conduct.

Aye, that, my friend, is indeed a true portrait of the religion of *reafon and nature*; and what pity it is that the world does not furniſh out a few more *deiſts* on that plan ?—There would then be a proportionally lefs occaſion for revelation.—But what ſhall we fay when nature, whilſt ſhe affords us fo ample a fyſtem of moral and religious duties, abounds at the fame time with fuch a group of fpecious allurements to recede from it ? What if men, if even *deiſts*, from the neceſſity of their conſtitution (as *degenerated* free agents I mean) are more liable to exceed, than to keep within, the bounds of their duty ? Did not fenfuality and voluptuoufnefs, did not envy, pride and ambition, too frequently uſurp the province of right reafon, the *religion of nature* would not ſtand fo much in need perhaps, as it now does, of the propofed aſſiſtances of *revelation*; but 'tis to remove thofe obſtructions to a proper exercife of the one, that the other comes in aid.

If therefore you would have me acquiefce in your opinion, that a *revealed religion* is fuperfluous and therefore not probable, you muſt firſt prove it to be fo by a difintereſted enquiry into the real truth of the cafe---by a ſtrict, *confiſtent* attention to your own golden rule, *the religion of reafon and nature.* The meer fuggeſtions of

your

your own fancy are of no moment at all in the affair, nor the prepo-
feffions you may have imbibed from another man's hafty and authoritative declaration. Thefe, added to the bias of your own
wifhes may eafily enough induce you to believe that revelation is
therefore indefenfible. But alas! how eafy a matter is it for a man
to believe that to be falfe, which he has either an inclination to fuppofe, or too much reafon to wifh, not to be true! If *the religion of reafon and nature* therefore my friend is the directory of *your* faith
and practice in life, try whether from thence you can deduce arguments fufficient to juftify a rejection of the Chriftian difpenfation;
fee whether from the light of the one you can difcover any thing
really unnatural in the purpofes from which originates the other.
Whether, in the firft place, it is in fact *not* agreeable to *reafon* to
fuppofe that nature (fallible as fhe appears to be) fhould receive
from time to time fuch admonitions and inftructions from the Deity,
as may be a probable means to forward her in the difcharge of her
various duty? And then, fecondly, whether revelation, having fo
apparently probability in its favour, can *reafonably* be treated with
derifion, infolence and contempt? If the principles on which your
deifm is fupported will countenance fuch a procedure as this, they
are but a fandy foundation for your confidence, carrying with them
a manifeft repugnancy to the very effence of *natural* religion, and
diffenting from it in a point *infinitely momentous.*

True, fay you, but what then? I am not (as I faid before) one
of thofe random contemners of revelation here fuppofed; I have
reafons for my infidelity, well examined, well confidered; and
(a point which muft neceffarily be fettled, e'er I can propofe yield-
ing up to you even any of my doubts and fcruples) have the
circumftance of *improbability* to oppofe to the *prefumptive evidences* of Chriftianity; the former greatly preponderating, as I appre-
hend, to the difadvantage of the *latter.*

For

For in the firſt place is not *the law of nature*, when attended to as it ought, (and with whom lies the fault if it is not) a full, ſufficient guide to our conduct ? Are we not prompted by the dictates of right reaſon, to act in a manner anſwerable to the end of our creation, and the dignity of human nature ? How prepoſterous is it then, as ſays a late eminent writer,* " for a man to hunt after a guide to his conduct, when the author of his being has planted one in his own breaſt. ?"

But under the ſuppoſed influence of ſuch an all-ſufficient guide to his judgment, how comes it that that writer ſhould with ſo little judgment oppoſe his own private opinion to the ſentiments of men unqueſtionably his *equals* at leaſt, if not his *ſuperiors*, in every advantage that learning, application, and even natural abilities, could give them ? How happened it that *he* was not inſtructed from *within*, to treat with more ſuitable reſpect a religion embraced and reverenced by thoſe, who were not more remarkable for their piety than for their parts and penetration ? And if the ſcriptures do really abound with ſuch inconſiſtencies and abſurdities, which he, from but a bare ſuperficial knowledge of them, is pleaſed to lay to their charge, how comes it that they ſhould have eſcaped the cenſure of a *Locke*, an *Addiſon*, a *Newton?* There is no reaſon to be given why *they* ſhould be *more* partial to any fancied failings of holy writ, than Mr. *Chubb*; but many, why the judgment they have given in its favour, ſhould be taken in preference to the calumnies and aſperſions with which *he* has thought fit to load it. Unleſs, as Dr. *Rogers* obſerves, learning, ſtudy, and all thoſe advantages which are uſually thought to render one man's judgment preferable to another's, are to be eſteemed, in the enquiry after truth, of no moment, of no conſideration whatſoever.

* Vid. Chubb's Farewel.

He ought to have confidered, that if fome have, with more ftubborn prefumption, perhaps, than felf-perfuafion, pronounced Chriftianity to be falfe, none have yet been able to make it appear fo to the conviction of fincere, impartial, and learned enquirers: and that it would have been worth the employment of his great *intellectual abilities,* to account for the conduct of the Supreme Being, in fuffering a deceit of that kind (if it be one) to pafs upon mankind through fo many ages paft, for feemingly no other end and purpofe, than to be the parent of the moft cruel miferies to its firft champions and defenders,——a fountain from whence flowed an ocean of innocent blood. For I think it ought to be particularly remarked, that if at any time falfe religions have been obtruded on mankind by the irrefiftible *authority* of the fword, none but ours has been eftablifhed on the more trying principle, a readinefs *to perifh with the fword*---none but ours has gained profelytes to its caufe, under fuch ftrong *prophetic* intimations of what unparallelled cruelties they were to encounter, who engaged in its defence. And if you can conceive it poffible, that men, acting under the moft pure and fervent piety towards God, fhould be given up by him to fuch a complicated feverity of fate, in confequence of opinions *really falfe and groundlefs,* you muft acknowledge, that they were of all men, as *unaccountably* as *undefervedly,* the moft miferable.

But to return.----That there is interwoven in our nature a directory to our conduct, which, would we attend to it, would fecure us from ever erring in our practice ; a rule for our judgment, to which if we would but appeal, we fhould be as feldom erroneous in our principles, I can readily enough admit. By the term confcience, we ufually diftinguifh the one ; right reafon, we call the other. Two different names, in fact, for one and the fame thing---It is the fitnefs of things which comprehends both. But is this fame law of nature fufficient, *in fact,* to keep men within the bounds

of

their complicated duty? Do men invariably act up to the rules which right reason prescribes?---That this is not the case, the several daily violations of the laws of society, too abundantly evince. And if in answer to that, it be said, that neither is revelation, with all its coercive authority, or most persuasive allurements, sufficient for these ends—what will follow? Why, that men are men, subject to the controul of passions to which they even court an obedience, and will gratify, when it is their inclination so to do, in opposition to the persuasions of either reason or revelation.

The only question meriting, my dear Sir, your attention, is which of the two is most likely to answer *now*, as a *directory* for man's conduct. *Reason*, subject as it is to the many inherent frailties and imperfections of human nature; or *revelation*, which comes in aid to it, and is proposed to us for the very purpose of *removing* those imperfections? From the appearance which the former now makes, we are apt to entertain a fallacious idea of its *native* endowments; not considering the advantages it has borrowed, and the education, if I may so speak, which it has in various instances received from that revelation which has furnished it from time to time with insights into the wondrous views of Divine Providence, impossible to have been attained *solely* by *human* penetration. And if you would but carry your thoughts back to those past times of wretchedness and despair, when a gathered cloud of darkness, ignorance and error, overshadowed the whole earth; you would surely cease to doubt the *occasion* of God's sending to us that day spring from on high to visit *us*. You would, on the contrary, be induced to acknowledge, with a becoming gratitude, the many essential advantages so happily derived to us from the seasonable event.

For

For as, by his fatal tranfgreffion, our firft parent had bereaved himfelf, in a great meafure, of that inward purity of nature, wherein he was created, and had contracted, in length of time, a general pronenefs to fin and wickednefs; it is not to be fuppofed, but that he muft tranfmit to his defcendants fome fhare at leaft of that deadly and diffufive poifon. And accordingly we find in fact, that the prefent generation of men (his offspring) are all born into the world, with a predominant bias towards evil, are become complexionally averfe to every thing that is good, and difpofed to a life of impiety, unrighteoufnefs, and fenfuality. And from the feveral hiftories of the heathen world we learn, that men, through a kind of gloomy and fullen defpair of divine mercy, arifing from a too confcious fenfe of their own unworthinefs, and varioufly contracted guilt, fell at length into a fettled indifference towards that God, on whofe deferved wrath and indignation they could not reflect but under the moft terrifying fears, and foreboding apprehenfions; till at length, fucceeding ages loft fight of both him and his laws; were fo far from perceiving, or even wifhing his regard for them, that they did not even choofe to retain him in their knowledge, but transferred the worfhip due to the only true God to an impious adoration of the meaneft of his creatures, even to birds and four footed beafts, and creeping things.

And if the wifer and more underftanding part of mankind, were not fo univerfally loft in ignorance and error, fo wholly abandoned to a proftituted worfhip and fervice; yet were *they* notwithftanding in a confeffedly wretched and difconfolate ftate. They were fenfible of their loft innocency, and of courfe forfeited intereft with their maker, of which their confciences too plainly reminded them; and, what muft confiderably awaken their fears and apprehenfions, could not frame to themfelves, any probable fcheme for re-inftating themfelves in his favour. They could eafily enough, by the light of nature alone, difcover the danger they were in of being punifhed for their bad conduct ; but could not, from any conclufions of reafon, affure themfelves, that, become, as was unhappily their cafe, obnoxious to God's juftice, that he would remit the punifhment due to their crimes, upon either the merit of their repentance, or any *piacular* oblations in their power to offer up to him, " though they gave their firft born for their tranfgreffion, the fruit of their body for the fin of their foul."

No, this was the great work reserved for our *Saviour* to accomplifh.—It was he, and he alone, who was to eafe them of their fears with refpect to that moft momentous concern, and be the happy inftrument of reconciling them to their offended God.---He it was whom God himfelf fent into the world to *fave finners*--- to preach to them a *remiffion* of fins, in an unlimited degree, (un-limited, I mean, as to the nature of their crimes) upon the limited, but rational terms of the Gofpel---In a word, there was wanting, fays a very fenfible and ufeful writer,* " there was wanting a re-velation to difcover, in what manner, and with what kind of exter-nal fervice, God might acceptably be worfhipped ;---there was wanting a revelation to difcover, what expiation he would be plea-fed to accept for fin, when his honour and authority were affront-ed ;---there was wanted a revelation to give man affurance of the great motives of religion---the rewards and punifhments of a fu-ture ftate ; in fine, there was wanting a particular revelation to make the whole doctrine of religion clear and obvious to all capa-cities ; to add weight and authority to the plaineft precepts ; and to furnifh men with extraordinary affiftances, to enable them to over-come the corruptions of their nature :---and without the affiftance

* *Vide Stackhoufe's* Body of divinity, *p.* 19.

of

fuch a revelation, their wifeft men were always of this opinion, that the world can never be reformed."

You may even give over, fays *Socrates*, all hopes of amending men's manners for the future, unlefs God be pleafed to fend you fome *other perfon to inftruct you:* for whatever is fet right, as fays *Plato*, in the prefent ill ftate of the world, can only be done by the interpofition of God.*

This, in fhort, is the multiplied bufinefs of revelation; this the great work begun by the *Abrahamic*, continued by the *Mofaic*, and completed by the *Chriftian* difpenfation.

Now if fuch a fuppofed circumftance in the divine œconomy, feems to you either impoffible or incredible ; if you think it an abfurdity in nature, to fuppofe that God fhould *fend* a perfon into the world purpofely to make difcoveries, merely and folely for the confolation and future happinefs of *his creatures*; that the perfon thus fent, fhould be enabled to work miracles in *teftimony* of his miffion, and at laft fuffer death to *accomplifh* the benign purpofe : if you fay all this *kind* of reafoning is amounting in fact to an abfurdity, and is therefore, with refpect to the fubject matter of it, really incredible, you muft difpute the merit of even *any* perfon's claim to an authority, the declared end or defign of which is, in nature, fo extraordinary, and, as you think, fo unwarranted.

But if reafon will not, cannot, authorife a diffidence fo derogatory to thofe moft unqueftionable attributes of the Divine Nature, his love, his tendernefs, and compaffion towards his creatures, in the one cafe here fuppofed, I know not how you can juftify an infinuation fo unfavourable to the dignity and divine authority afíumed by Jefus Chrift, intimated and implied in the other.

* *Vide Plato*, in Apol. Socrat.

That

That there was actually born into the world such a person as Jesus Christ, we have at least the same rational evidence for believing, as that there ever existed an *Alexander*, or *Julius Cæsar*. That that same *Jesus* did also work frequent miracles, not even his enemies could deny ; though they were pleased, sometimes to ascribe them to the agency of *Beelzebub*, the prince of devils. That he was *there-fore*, fully authorized to demand our attention to those several doctrines exhibited to us in his Gospel, as truths delivered by the will and approbation of God (a point now *secondly* to be considered) we are sufficiently encouraged to believe from the following plain and obvious conclusion of right reason : the only argument on this point to which I shall request your attention at present.

It is a truth, I think incontestible, that our Saviour could not work miracles, in support of doctrines so unquestionably good and useful, as are those which characterize the precepts of the Gospel, but by the concurrent agency of a good spirit *necessarily residing in*, or immediately *derived* to him, from the fountain of goodness himself. In either case, it is quite consistent with the dictates of right reason, to attend to the miracles, on account of the doctrines ; and to pay a regard to the doctrines, in deference to the miracles.

I am not insensible with what raillery this maxim is treated by many, who term it arguing in a circle ; yet am I not, therefore, the less satisfied of its force, propriety, and usefulness. For if, at any time, men's attention to a train of truths, not so naturally obvious and intelligible, perhaps, as necessary and important, could be best and most effectually engaged by an awful display of some unusual, some miraculous testimonies of those truths : it is far from being incredible, that such expedients should occasionally have been employed to so noble, generous, and useful an end. But will it as naturally follow, that God should at any time direct, or even

permit

permit the uſe of ſuch *extraordinary* means of working upon men's ſenſes and paſſions, barely to miſlead them into error? That invariable principle of univerſal love and benevolence, which gave birth to, and is, as it were, the very ſoul of creation itſelf, will ever reſtrain its Divine Author from reverſing, or ſuffering others to reverſe the *natural* to the deſtruction of the *moral* government of the world. Nor can any of thoſe ſtated laws of nature, by which is regulated, with ſuch conſummate wiſdom, each diſtinct ſyſtem in the grand *univerſal whole*, ever be interrupted, but by virtue of a power adequate to, or in part and on purpoſe communicated from that which at firſt eſtabliſhed them. So that miracles muſt ever come with a greater or leſs degree of credibility, in proportion to the appeal made to them, in proof of a greater or leſs *univerſal* utility.

Nor will the confident report of other miracles, which ſeem to be urged only in ſupport of doctrines in themſelves falſe or frivolous, diſcredit in the leaſt the teſtimony of thoſe wrought by our Saviour, in evidence of what is true and important—with men, I mean, who are willing to diſtinguiſh truth from falſehood—what is, from what is not—with men, in ſhort, who can proportion, properly, their aſſent to the ſeveral different degrees of credibility with which atteſted facts come attended. For two or more recorded miracles may come ſupported by the ſame *external* circumſtances of credibility, and yet they may not be *therefore* all equally, all *internally* alike credible. A fit occaſion for every *ſuppoſed* miraculous interpoſition of Divine Power, ſhould be firſt proved, e'er we give a willing aſſent to even the moſt plauſible evidence brought in favour of it;

Nec Deus interſit niſi dignus vindice nodus
Inciderit.   HOR.

This

This confideration, added to the known completion of prophecies, which adds a degree of probability to the recorded miracles of our Saviour and his apoftles, with which none others come attended, is what gives that partial but honeft bias to our faith in *them*, preferably and in contradiction to all others of a more modern date.

Point me out fome doctrine fairly deducible from thofe miracles afcribed to Abbé *Paris*; a doctrine evidently claimant of fo extraordinary a token of the divine fanction; a doctrine of real confequence to the prefent and future happinefs of mankind; and which they could not have arrived to the knowledge of, but by fome actual *immediate* intelligence from the Deity; and I fhould be cautious how I difputed the veracity of the reports given of them. But when, on the other hand, the reverfe is more evidently the real cafe, it concerns me not to make them at all a fubject of my enquiry. If they would influence men to views and practices difcountenanced and condemned by laws natural or revealed, I, in that cafe, may reafonable conclude, that there is fome latent impenetrable juggle in the affair; and in fact, that they are no *miracles* at all; but fuch lying wonders, only, as have been frequently *foretold*, and might poffibly be effected by the cunning craftinefs of men interefted in cafting a mift before the eyes of thofe who loved darknefs rather than light; and whofe fubtilty might be fufficient to deceive even the *elect*.

Not to dwell, therefore, unneceffarily long on a point of enquiry, in itfelf of fo *little* moment, on only *imaginary* difadvantages to the important caufe of Chriftianity; without dwelling upon thofe feveral previous difpenfations of God's providence, introductory to the miffion of *Jefus* in the fullnefs of time; the wonderful preparation with which it was introduced, *viz.* a long train of preliminary incidents; direct promifes to the ancient patriarchs; a va-

riety

ricty of prophetic intimations, both before and under the legal œconomy; and laftly, an exprefs declaration, that He (by name)
fhould come fo and fo qualified and circumftanced in life as did
our Saviour, I fay, waving thefe corroborating evidences of a divine fanction, which might be urged in further evidence of the
facred character he affumed; it may be fufficient, I prefume, to
conclude, from his power of working miracles, in fupport of doctrines fo evidently good and ufeful as were thofe recorded in his
Gofpel, that Jefus Chrift was that *anointed* of Heaven whom we
are *called upon* to *hear* and of courfe, to *believe* and obey *in all things
whatfoever he faith unto us.*

Well, allowing, for argument fake, the *probability* of God's
having actually revealed himfelf (by means of the Gofpel of Jefus
Chrift) for the information, comfort, and future happinefs of mankind, yet, fhew me, fay you, in the *third* place, the genuinenefs of
thofe writings, which are faid to be fuch a faithful repofitory of that
fame revelation, and their expediency to anfwer thofe very purpofes for which they are prefumed to be intended.

How, in the firft place, does it appear, that the Scriptures are
really the writings of thofe very perfons, under whofe names they
are publifhed, or, that the feveral circumftances therein related,
were evidenced by real matters of fact?

Why, all this I believe, upon thofe grounds of credibility, which
challenge my belief of the authenticity and genuinenefs of any other
book or hiftory you fhall name me.—But are writings, fay you,
in which are faid to be concerned the falvation of mankind, to
be put upon the fame footing with books which contain in them little
more, perhaps, than mere matters of amufement? Is it of the fame
                                                        confequence,

confequence, whether thofe hiftories, in which are recorded the exploits of a *Cæfar* and an *Alexander*, are true and genuine relations, as the hiftory of our Saviour and his apoftles ?—No, that be far from me to infinuate. But then, unlefs you can think it reafonable to difregard all faith in hiftory, as a point of credulity in itfelf abfurd and unwarrantable, and will infift upon it, that nothing in fact is to be believed, but what we ourfelves fee done before our eyes ; I would afk you, how things tranfacted at a confiderable diftance of time paft, whether of facred ftory or prophane, can be tranfmitted to pofterity, but through the fame kind of channel ? What other methods need be ufed, to engage our confidence in the one, than are neceffary to eftablifh the credit and authority of the other? Or by what *arguments* you would endeavour to convince me, that *Livy* and *Herodotus* were in reality the authors of thofe hiftories which go, with fuch unqueftioned pretenfions, under their names, and that the accounts given by each, have, as hiftorical narrations, a proper evidence to fupport them, which will not lie with equal weight, in either of thofe particulars, in favour of the hiftories of both the Old and New Teftament?

Well—fuppofing that to be a confideration, as much in proof, as you would wifh, in the firft place of the *authenticity* of the Scriptures in general, yet wherein, fay you, confifts their *importance* in point of *information* and *inftruction ?* For how fhall I know where, among fuch a variety of readings in the fame book, to fix upon that which is the true one ?—Why, the fame rules of criticifm which you would make ufe of, to difcover the true reading of any one author among the claffics at large, muft be employed in your perufal and examination of thefe. In either cafe, your reafon (as far as you have qualified it for paffing judgment upon a matter of fuch *effential* import by thofe ufual affiftances, which enable a man to become a critic in any other learned *compofition* what-

D   foever)

foever) muft be your guide. If at any time, in the courfe of your enquiries, doubts and difficulties arife, which you yourfelf cannot mafter, you muft, in order to their being fet in a true and proper light, have recourfe to, and depend on, in proportion to their fuperior fkill and acquirements, the judgment of others. And unlefs you would conclude, becaufe various have been the readings of *Homer*, of *Virgil*, and of *Horace*, and contradictory accounts given by eftablifhed hiftorians, that therefore neither of them are to be regarded as genuine and eftablifhed writers, or as authors deferving our perufal, I will defire you to put it home to your breaft, and ingenuoufly tell me, whether you think there is, in reality, any foundation for impeaching the facred writings of non-authenticity and integrity, of infufficiency as a rule of faith, or of unwarranted pretenfions, as a repofitory of revealed truths—becaufe *they* have accidentally given occafion to a variety of diffonant readings and interpretations?

But who, fay you, in the difficult cafes fuppofed above, are the judges by which I am at laft to be determined, when among thofe very perfons, who claim an *authority* to preach and expound fcripture doctrines, fo few, even among thefe, agree in giving the fame unvaried meaning to the fame paffages and expreffions in thofe admired pages?

A queftion is here fuppofed, which may be beft anfwered by the following important piece of advice: it is this—

After having thoroughly examined the grounds and evidences of *Chriftianity*, make the due diftinction between *that* and the *pretended* truths charged upon it. Make yourfelf mafter of every argument which points out the divine authority of our Saviour; and when that is done, attend clofely to the feveral doctrines he

4   advances

advances as an *appointed* revealer of the will of Heaven. What *He* says you will, of courfe, in deference to that *authority* with which he *fpeaks*, receive and believe. What *others* fay *for* him, or affert *of* him, by virtue of *their* commiffion and infpired powers, *that* claims, *in proportion*, the fame regard. So that thofe doctrines which our Saviour delivered concerning the Father, himfelf, and all mankind, or the apoftles, in his name, are by all means to be embraced without referve——Thus far fhalt thou go, and no far-ther—I mean, for faith neceffarily *undefiled*——For practice you may go farther; from the Scriptures you may repair to thofe ve-nerable lights, the *fathers*, for edification, for difcipline, for patterns of fanctity and moral purity—There you have before you an un-bounded field of inftruction.

But if, through an excefs of pious zeal, *they* would, at any time, carry you into matters of faith (or practice) not warranted either by reafon or revelation, there, if you are wife, you will take your leave of them: for though we are not to confider them in that ridiculous light, in which a late eminent writer* has penciled them out to the world, yet neither are we to view them through the medium of *in-fallibility*. They claim from us much for their tranfmitted records of primitive ftory; much for their exemplary piety and devotion; much for their unfhaken conftancy and Chriftian fortitude. Let us, however, not be afraid to acknowledge, that they *cafually* fhared weakneffes and imperfections in common with the reft of mankind. And when thefe are made the fubject of ridiculous banter by fome, let us not be under fuch an alarm, as if, with *theirs*, thofe *fathers* I mean, the reputation of *Chriftianity* is proportionally endangered. The reafonings of thofe pious fages are at beft but the reafonings of *men*. All doctrines therefore deduced by *them* from Scripture, which are not apparently *profitable* for *edification* as well as *inftruction*, may reafonably be confidered as coming with fo *queftionable* a claim

* The late Dr. Middleton.

to

to our attention, that neither, if we believe them, are we better, neither, if we believe them not, are we the worfe.

But will you, becaufe difputes may have run high on fome topics of enquiry, weakly or wickedly termed *Chriftian*, conclude, that therefore our genuine *unfophifticated* code of religion is in the grofs, to be difregarded ? *Your* boafted *religion of nature*, in which there is fcarce any one principle which has not been made the fubject of difpute, may, by a parity of reafon, be rejected alfo. " Has not the exiftence of a God, the liberty of man, the nature of good and evil; what is happinefs ; what it is that thinks within us ; whether the foul be material or immaterial, mortal or immortal ; the nature of juftice and moral honefty ; in fhort, every point of morality or natural religion, been controverted ? Is the inference from thence, that there is or can be no fuch thing as natural religion ? Is there no fuch thing as truth, becaufe the queftion has been, what is truth ? Is there no fuch thing as right reafon, becaufe men have maintained infinite abfurdities and contradictions about every thing in even matters of moral obligation ?"*

But would not Providence, fay the Deifts, have prevented the Scriptures from becoming fuch a fource of various fentiments and opinions, if he had intended them for that general and important benefit we imagine ? Would he not have left us fuch an unerring criterion, for afcertaining a right interpretation of the *facred pages* throughout, as that all who have the fame opportunities and qualifications for confulting them, muft neceffarily unite in giving to the fame paffages and expreffions the fame meaning ?

If this is reafonably to be expected from *revelation*, as a *guide*, I would afk, why it happens, that under the fuppofed *infallible*

---

* Vid. Dr. Benfon, on the Reafonablenefs of Chriftianity.

direction

direction of *right reason*, any two in life are capable of differing in point of judgment in even matters of meer moral obligation ? A suppofed infallibility in the *writers* of revealed truths, does not neceffarily preclude the natural fallibility of their feveral *readers*. The unerring *directrix*, in fhort, for difcerning either the authority of the gofpel difpenfation, or the doctrines feverally deducible from it, is abfolutely and folely *right reafon*. But whilft different men of different views, prejudices, and prepoffeffions, fubftitute in its ftead *opinion*, it is no wonder, if many others are betrayed into a complaint, that no fixed rule at all is given us for that purpofe.

I hope, by this time, that my friend accedes to the force of *reafon*, and is convinced, that a Deift, in order to his thinking and acting agreeably to the *religion of reafon and nature*, is under an indifpenfable obligation to be a friend to, and efpoufe with fincerity, the religion of Jefus Chrift ; and for this reafon, becaufe *that* coming to us as a promulgation of divine truths and inftructions, lays evidently as great a claim to our notice and efteem, as any moral obligation whatfoever. Nor is it my friend, an argument of any weight, which fome urge againft the probability of a fuppofed *revealed* religion, that the moral duties it means to enforce, are none elfe than what natural reafon recommends : this fhould ferve rather to ftrengthen than weaken its authority ; fince to thofe inftinctive impulfes of *nature* which Chriftianity recommends to our regard, it fuperadds as well proper motives as proper means, to engage us in the practice of them. To name no more at prefent with regard to the latter, than the duties of *examination, mortification,* and *felf-denial,* which are indifputably fuch points of difcipline, as all, who impartially confider them, will acknowledge to be eftablifhed upon views truly rational, and univerfally ferviceable.

So

So far confidered then it muſt appear very evident, I think, to the impartial, that a rejection of revelation is not authoriſed by the *religion of reaſon and nature* ; or the cauſe of *Deiſm* in the leaſt advantaged by a ſuppoſition, " That *Socrates*, and thoſe of old, were as great ornaments, and did as much honour to human nature, as any *Chriſtian* ever did."

Had it been ſaid, that *Socrates*, &c. did as much honour, and were as great ornaments to human nature, ſo circumſtanced as it was in *their* days, as *Chriſtians* do and are now, to the improved religion, and other ſuperior advantages *they* pride themſelves in the poſſeſſion of, there had been perhaps too much truth in the remark. But if they mean to infer from that conceſſion, which moſt aſſuredly they do, that nothing more is required of *us*, in point of moral and religious obligations, than, beſides copying thoſe worthies of old in their practice, to attend with a becoming conſcientious deference to their precepts, they undoubtedly miſlead their followers into a moſt palpable and fatal error. They, in that caſe, either weakly or wickedly deceive them. They muſt either not know what are the grand extenſive purpoſes of revelation, and then their random aſperſions on it are an argument of a moſt unpardonable wantonneſs of impiety, a prejudging irreverence of behaviour towards its divine author ; or they muſt knowingly and wilfully miſrepreſent them---and then I would aſk how ſuch a conduct quadrates with the dictates of the *religion of reaſon and nature*.

They cannot be under any the leaſt degree of doubt, but that the deſign of Chriſtianity is to make ſuch diſcoveries as ſhould, and if duly attended to, would lead to actions more ſuitably good and rational, than were before in *general* practice ; to inforce the obligation

gation of moral duties, by ſtronger and more perſuaſive motives than the religion of nature *depraved*—than even the religion and improved ſentiments of *Socrates* could, with any proper *authority*, eſtabliſh ; and to complete men for attainments for which they were created.

The religion of old (totally devoid of thoſe ſtrong enforcements to the practice of the law of nature, with which Chriſtianity abounds) furniſhed out ſuch intimations concerning the nature of things as were either very doubtful, dark, and obſcure, or elſe conſpicuouſly weak, whimſical, and abſurd—Witneſs their many extravagant conceptions of the firſt cauſe all things and the nature and origin of man ; their confuſed ideas of the formation and government of the world, and their ſtill more inconſiſtent views and practices in the courſe of their *religious* forms and ceremonies, which were diſtinguiſhed by either a ſolemn ſeries of idolatrous impiety, or, if I my ſo ſpeak, by a courſe of *pious* inhumanity, by their either *worſhipping ſtocks* and *ſtones*, or *offering up their ſons and daughters unto devils.*

The intended redemption of mankind, from the guilt and miſery they were too conſcious of having contracted ; the doctrine of a reſurrection from the dead, of a judgment to come, and of rewards and puniſhments in an after-ſtate, are verities, which if men ever arrived to any tolerable degree of knowledge concerning them, vaniſhed from the world a long time before the coming of our Saviour—Nor does it appear, that life and immortality were ever clearly brought to light, but by the Goſpel : No, not by the all-penetrating *Socrates,* or even the divine *Plato* himſelf. The *nature* and *terms,* however, of the *redemption,* the *perſon* by whom it was to be effected, and by whom the world is at laſt

to

to be judged, were circumstances of information, in their nature, not capable of being derived to men, but through the channel of *revelation.*

But if *Socrates* was confirmed in the belief of some of these truths, yet could *he* make them equally apparent to others ? Could he publish them to the world with that degree of confidence and authority, as did our *Saviour*; who, by a series of miracles, prophecies, and an unspotted conduct in life, gave sufficient evidence to the *impartial*, of a derived commission from *Heaven*, to declare, confirm, and establish them ?

And if, after all, you could prove to me, that moral obligations, to which *Socrates* is presumed so remarkably to have attended, and which we will *suppose* him so illustriously to have discharged, work so universally strong and powerfully on men's consciences, as that they naturally perform what they see or know to be their duty, I would grant you, that then nothing more would seem needful, as a law to their conduct, than the awakening voice of nature and right reason. But since daily experience evinces, that men want more to be excited to the practice of their duty, than to be informed wherein it consists, it is evident, that revelation, if only on account of its many *peculiar motives* to virtue, is *therefore* highly eligible, and *worthy of all acceptation.* For what can we conceive more necessary and important, more conducive to the safety and well-being of society, than to solicit men's attention to, among others, the important duties of integrity, piety, temperance, chastity, and charity on the principles of *Christian* obedience ; Of what general advantage, I say, must it be, to have these duties *enforced* on the consciences of men, by the added hopes and terrors of a day to come, when *God will bring every work into judgment, with every secret thing, whether it be good, or whether it be evil.*

But

and terrors of a day to come, when *God will bring every work into judgment, with every secret thing, whether it be good, or whether it be evil.*

But to proceed.—Our Deift, in page the fixth, gives us a notable fpecimen of his dexterity in forging, on occafion, the ftamp of *authority* on the Deift's principles, in order to make them pafs with a more fpecious fplendid currency through the world; and the inftance I am going to give of it, ferves, at the fame time to fhew, with what eagernefs and affiduity the Deifts will catch at every the fmalleft twig they can meet with in their way, to fave a finking caufe; the great name *he* has been pleafed, in the following cafe, to make free with, being ever before univerfally diftinguifhed by principles as diffimilar to his own, as light is to darknefs, or orthodoxy to infidelity.

Dr. *Sherlock*, if you will believe our Deift, is one of thofe rational divines who afferts, "that Deifm is the only excellency and true glory of Chriftianity." (p. 6.)—If he had confulted the bifhop with any other view than by laying hold of fome detached, disjointed paffages in his fermon,* to make it fpeak, if poffible, with fome feeming approbation of *his* fcheme of thinking, he would, I am perfuaded, have found, in inftances without number, that his Lordfhip and he think as differently of revelation, as a believer and an unbeliever *can* think.

" The religion of the Gofpel, fays the Bifhop, is the true original religion of reafon and nature.+" And again, " the Gofpel has reference to the law of reafon and nature :"—and what of all

* Sermon for propagating the Gofpel in foreign parts.

+ Vid. Dr. Leland, p. 42.

that ?

that? Is the Bifhop a *Deift* on the evidence of thefe declarations? If he is not, to what purpofe is he quoted? And if he is, mark the confequence to our author.

Dr. *Sherlock* fays, and our *Deift* himfelf *approves* the affertion, " that the religion of the Gofpel is the true original religion of reafon and nature." Aye! what this from a Deift? Alas! our Deift, like a confufed culprit at the *Old Bailey*, cites a t once a fancied friend to his character, without confidering that the man was too honeft not to fay what he thought; and that the evidence he muft give, would but aggravate and add weight to the profecution.

Here the bifhop is called in, to vouch for our author's rationality as a Deift. 'Well, and how does he prove it? Why, by afferting, that that revelation which the Deift *derides*, is nothing fhort of the religion of reafon and nature, which he pretends to approve——Our author for your man of *found judgment and nervous reafoning!*

Our Deift having here then, a little unluckily for himfelf, cited a paffage from Dr. *Sherlock*, which proves too plainly, that his oppofition to Chriftianity is equally repugnant to the principles of *natural reafon and religion,* is forced at laft to add, by way of fupplement to his Lordfhip's own words, confcious how inexpreffive they were before to his advantage, or rather, how expreffive to his confufion, fomething, though full as little to his purpofe, from the product of his own brain.

After telling us that Dr. *Sherlock* fays, " it is true, that there are fome inftitutions in the Gofpel, which, in their own nature, are no *conftituent parts of religion,*" I will venture to add, fays he, " that the fame may be faid, for ought that appears to the contrary, of

fome

fome *doctrines* of the Gofpel, which doctrines, together with the inftitutions referred to, may be faid to conftitute pure Chriftianity, by
way of contradiftinction to pure *natural* religion." *(p.* 6.) So that
according to the very modeft reafoning of our Deift, what confti-
tutes pure Chriftianity in the grofs, is an abfolute and entire oppofition in all its parts, in its precepts, ceremonies, and doctrines, to the
very being of *natural religion*; and that thofe inftitutions, and ceremonies, and doctrines, and thofe only which are no conftituent
parts of natural religion, do collectively make up the fum total of
Chriftianity. Was this in reality the cafe, was Chriftianity in fact
fo unreafonable, I will add, fo *irreligious* an inftitution, I would
myfelf join our author in condemning and rejecting it; or, with
Mr. *Chandler* agree, that it would then be fcarce worth while to
enquire what the religion of Chrift is. *(p.* 7.)

But what if after all it appears, that thofe very inftitutions, ceremonies, and doctrines, which conftitute pure Chriftianity, are the
inftitutions, the ceremonies, and the doctrines, which abfolutely
conftitute the Religion of *Reafon and Nature*—proportionally
I mean, and as parts to the whole? For you muft obferve, that
I regard every fubfervient *inftrument* of *religion*, as a material part of
religion itfelf. That a public worfhip of God therefore is not lefs
a part of the *religion of reafon and nature*, than any pofitive precept
of the Gofpel, our Deift cannot aim to difprove, without oppofing,
at the fame time, the general fenfe and practice of all ages paft;
there being no people, of any religion whatfoever, but what always exprefled in a *public* manner their veneration of the deities
they owned, by fuch external tokens of reverence, as were moft in
ufe am ong them.*

---

* Scott's Works, vol. II. p. 130. fol. edit.

" *Lactantius,*

" *Lactantius*, as an argument of the abſurdity of *polytheiſm*, ſuppoſes it an univerſal conceſſion among men, that they ſhould pay to *each* God, whom they acknowledged, divine worſhip : and this not only in honour of his divinity, but in conſideration of his *paternity*, as *that* one common parent, from whom they received life, health, and food.+" And of ſuch conſequence to the happi-neſs of a ſtate, ſays *Tully*, is piety towards the Gods, " that take away that, and you undermine the very foundations on which in-tegrity, friendſhip, and that moſt excellent of all virtues, juſtice it-ſelf, is ſupported.‡" And if we would endeavour, ſays *Wool-laſton*, to behave ourſelves towards God according to truth, we ſhall find ourſelves bound to worſhip him in the beſt manner we can. By worſhipping him, I mean, ſays he, owning him to be what he is, and ourſelves to be what we are, by ſome moſt ſo-lemn and proper act ; that is, by addreſſing ourſelves to him as his dependents, and as the ſupreme cauſe and governor of the world, with acknowledgments of what we enjoy, petitions for what we really want, or he knows to be convenient for us.*

And yet how can a plan of public worſhip, with any proprie-ty, any decency, be executed but by ſome ſuch viſible obſervances, ſome ſuch outward religious actions and declarations, which the wiſdom of Chriſtian ſocieties ſhall adjudge to be moſt expreſſive of that internal faith, love, and obedience, to which they are called by

+ Omnem Deum qui ab homine colitur neceſſe eſt inter ſolennes ritus et preca-tiones patrem nuncupari, non tantum honoris gratia verum etiam rationis quod et antiquior eſt homine, et quod vitam ſalutem victum præxſtat ut pater. *Lactant. de verâ ſap. et relig. lib. IV. p.* 177.

‡ Pietate adverſus Deos ſublata fides etiam et ſocietas humani generis, et excel-lentiſſima virtus juſtitia tollitur. *Cic. de nat. deor.*

* *Woollaſton*'s Religion of Nature.

their

their *religion*; and what are moft likely to kindle in each other's breafts a lively and lafting fenfe of piety, devotion, and every virtue? Inftead therefore of difregarding thefe neceffary appendages to public worfhip, as *no conflituent parts* of religion; as mere niceties and trifles, of no manner of confideration in the fight of God (as do avowedly too many of the feveral *feperatifts* from our communion) men fhould confider, whether they have or have not an apparent view to the known purpofes of religion; whether outward actions, which are fo many prefumptive evidences of inward difpofitions to piety and virtue in individuals, are not likely to promote the fame worthy affections in the community at large? And whether, in proportion to the importance of the end, we are not to regard the *means* conducive to that end?

As for thofe two *facramental* duties of our profeffion, viz. *Baptifm* and the *Lord's Supper*—Are they not, let me afk, inftitutions, folemn, rational, and morally inftructive? Do they not ferve to raife our devotions, to inflame our gratitude, to infufe *generous* fentiments? A queftion which thofe beft can anfwer, for thofe only know, who have perfonally *ratified* the one, and been *ferioufly* participant of the other. Be pleafed, however, if it be not a fubject too grave to engage your attention, to take an opinion of both, from the learned Dr. *Jenkins.*

" One of the purpofes, fays he, for which facraments were in-
" ftituted, was to be the outward and vifible fign of our entrance
" into covenant with him. For if covenants between man and
" man be made with all the formality of witneffes of hands, and
" feals and delivery, in folemn and exprefs words; if men know
" themfelves too well to truft one another, without this folem-
" nity, it may well be expected, that when God is pleafed to per-
" mit them to enter into covenant with himfelf, he fhould not re-
" ceive them under lefs obligations of caution and fecurity for their

" integrity, than men are wont to ufe among one another; fince
" every breach of covenant with him is infinitely more affronting
" and finful, than any breach of covenant with man can be. And
" as their outward figns ferve to raife our attentions and fix our
" minds, and fo put us in remembrance, that heaven and earth, an-
" gels and men, are witneffes againft us, if we prove treacherous
" and unfaithful in this covenant; fo they are as tokens and
" pledges to us of God's love and favour, and give us fenfible
" and vifible affurances of that grace which is invifible and fpi-
" ritual. 'Tis not a little in the nature and temper of man, to
" be better pleafed and contented with fomething prefent in hand,
" though of fmall value, and infignificant in itfelf, as a token and
" pledge of what is made over to him, than with the greateft pro-
" mifes and proteftations, without any thing as an earneft to con-
" firm them. Now, what is inward and invifible, is abfent as to
" fenfe, and what is future ftands in need of fomething prefent
" to reprefent it to us; and therefore God, who was pleafed to
" bind himfelf, as it were, by an oath, that he might be want-
" ing in nothing which might help our infirmities, and affift our
" faith, has been pleafed, for our comfort and truft in him, to
" appoint vifible figns and pledges of that which is invifible, and
" to give fuch affurance to our very fenfes, as they are capable
" of, that all the promifes of his fpiritual bleffings, fhall be as
" certainly fulfilled to us, as the outward figns and pledges are
" duly received by us; that the foul, even in this cafe, where it is
" more immediately concerned, might not be wholly independent
" on the body; but fince both muft be happy or miferable toge-
" ther in the next world, both might be affiftant in the way and
" means of falvation in this."

And to fhew the moral influence which the ufe of thefe facraments has naturally on our minds, the fame author obferves, of
" baptifm,

baptifin, that " it is a very fignificant and apt reprefentation of the
" cleanfing and puryfying the foul from fin; and that in this,
" men of all nations and all religicns feem to have been agreed.
" For nothing was more frequent among the heathens, than their
" wafhings and purifyings, and though they attributed a great
" deal too much to them, yet the fuperftitious opinions which
" they had of thefe outward cleanfings, could never have fo uni-
" verfally prevailed, if there had not been fome foundation for
" the ufe of them, in the nature of things; and that is, the great
" fitnefs which is in thofe outward wafhings, to excite us to pu-
" rity of mind, and to reprefent the great duty which lies upon us,
" to keep our confciences undefiled, which only can render us ac-
" ceptable to God.

And of the Lord's Supper he obferves, that " the elements of
" bread and wine have a peculiar fuitablenefs, to bring to our
" *remembrance* the body and blood of Chrift, offered upon the
" crofs for us, to make us partakers of them, to become the
" commemorative and reprefentat ve figns of the euchariit, and to
" be pledges of all the benefits which we receive thereby.* It is,
" as Dr. *Scott* obferves, a folemn commemoration of Chrift's
" death, and is an expreffion of kindnefs, fufficient to captivate
" the moft ungrateful fouls, and extort obedience from them; it
" is a fœderal right, whereby God and we, by feafting as it were
" together, do, according to the antient cuftom of Jews and Hea-
" thens, mutually engage ourfelves one to another, whereby God,
" by giving us the myftical bread and wine, and we by receiving
" them, do mutually engage ourfelves to one another, upon thofe
" facred pledges of Chrift's body and blood, that we will faithfully
" perform each their part of that everlafting covenant, which was

* Vide *Jenkins's* Reafonablenefs of the Chriftian Religion, *Stackhoufe's* Body of
Divinity.

" purchafed

" purchafed by Chrift; and what can be a greater reftraint to us,
" when we are folicited to any fin, than the fenfe of being un-
" der fuch a dreadful vow and obligation? With what face dare
" we liften to any temptation to evil, when we remember how
" lately we folemnly engaged ourfelves to the contrary, and took
" the facrament upon it?"†

If at any time thefe eftablifhed mementos to our conduct fail
having the intended influence on our morals; it is, becaufe the defign of each is not fo fufficiently attended to as to operate with the
proper impreffions of gratitude on our hearts. The remembrance
of that God, to whom we have devoted ourfelves in baptifm, paf-
feth away perhaps from off our mind, as the remembrance of a
gueft that tarrieth but a day; and the *cup of bleffing* is too frequently taken from our lips, as if we only *drank* to one; that cup
which, inftead of being a proper teft of our averfion to thofe fins
which occafioned Chrift's death, is—alas! how oft made only an
occafional introduction to an opportunity of profecuting them in
higher life.

But religion, fays a diftinguifhed advocate for Deifm,* is a matter purely perfonal, and the knowledge of it to be obtained by perfonal confiderations, independent of any guides, teachers, or ceremonies. An obfervation which, however confidently urged, will,
I am perfuaded, then only hold good, when there ceafe to be fuch
men in the world as he who firft advanced it—If human nature
was really in fuch a ftate of perfection, as that every man left to
himfelf, would reafon juftly, judge truly, and ever act with propriety, there would be little occafion not only for revelation, but for

† Vide *Scott's* Chriftian Life, vol. I, p. 115.

* Author of the Scheme of Literal Prophecy.

any

any *eſtabliſhed* laws, governments, or civil authority whatever in the world. But men, taken in the groſs, are, and ever will be, weak, ignorant, paſſionate, and conceited ; and muſt therefore be regulated by *juridical* authority of ſome kind or other.*

With what conſiſtent goodneſs therefore has the Deity interpoſed an authoritative declaration of his will, in a matter of ſuch mighty importance (which *none* can claim a right to diſpute) and given a law to our conduct in the great points of piety and morality, which cut off all *reaſonable* occaſions for doubts or difficulties in either!

. The great uſe and intent of all the enjoined poſitive duties and ceremonies of our religion, are obvious enough to all thoſe who examine them with fairneſs and impartiality ; nor do any of its doctrinal points, when not miſinterpreted and miſapplied, convey any ſenſe and meaning, which right reaſon will not allow to be rational objects of our faith, and, in proportion, *conſtituent* parts of religion. They not only afford us ſuch noble diſcoveries concerning the nature of the Deity, the origin of the univerſe, the great, the important plan of redemption, as were not ſufficiently developed by the painful reſearches of philoſophers of the moſt penetrating genius, but propoſe to us, at the ſame time, a ſyſtem of *morality* which ſurpaſſes all that comes recommended either by a *Lycrgus*, a *Numa*, a *Plato*, an *Ariſtotle*, &c. And would men examine the reaſonableneſs of the doctrines and moral precepts of the Goſpel, with coolneſs and impartiality, by the unerring teſt of ſober reaſon and reflection, and not by the treacherous direction of their depraved wills and affections, they would at once acknowledge, that to *love God with all our heart, with all our ſoul, and with all our ſtrength,*

* *Rogers's* Preface to his Vindication of the Chriſtian Religion.

F

is but a juft debt of gratitude to our Maker, for thofe numberlefs bleffings, we are every moment receiving from his all bountiful hand; and as the God and Author of nature is *holy*, that it fhould be our ftudy to be *holy in all manner of converfation*; that again, if we would pafs through the waves of a troublefome world, with a chearful and ferene mind, we muft be *patient*, under the afflicting hand of Heaven (whofe will we know to be an irrefiftable law) and refign up our wifhes to his fovereign pleafure, in confidence of that tendernefs which we know he bears to every individual of his creation.

As to thofe precepts of Chriftianity, which feem to bear the hardeft upon human nature, viz. *repentance and reftitution, mortification and felf-denial, humility, contentment and refignation, forgiving,* yea, and *loving* your enemies; what are thefe, when rightly confidered, but injunctions highly reafonable in themfelves, and fubfervient to our real happinefs? What can be more reafonable than forrow, or a repentant anguifh of mind, for offences more immediately committed againft God, or reftitution and retaliation for injuries we have at any time offered towards men? What more reafonable and advantageous, than that we fhould mortify and fubdue thofe fatal and rebellious lufts, which dare oppofe the dictates of right reafon, which would intice us into a violation of the laws of virtue and integrity, and fubject us to the vengeance of an angry God? And humility, is not *that* a prudent, laudable, and advantageous fpecies of conduct? That reputation or refpect, which is the fupreme ambition of *all*, how furely is it the portion of the affable, meek, and humble only! And then for thofe *pacific* virtues, of rendering good for evil, forgiving injuries, and even loving our enemies, how notorious is it, in their behalf, that they ever appear to the advantage of thofe who are eminent in the practice of them! How mollifying and attractive! how preventive of thofe many

reftlefs

reftlefs tumults, which are ever harraffing the minds of the revenge-
ful and malicious! What then will follow ? Why, that all thofe
inftitutions, ceremonies, and doctrines, which conftitute pure
Chriftianity, demand our utmoft reverence and efteem ; that we
do not act up to the *religion of reafon and nature*, when we dare to
treat them with *contempt, neglect* or *indifference*; and that if *you*
would be a rationalift, not in fpeculation only, but in practice;
you muft add to the virtues of mere *morality*, the faith and principles of Chriftianity : unlefs it appears that thofe writings from
whence we draw our belief as Chriftians, are a cheat and im-
pofition on mankind. If they come in fact with that authority
we afcribe to them, the very dictates of *natural religion* challenge
our regard to them ; and that they do not, it is at your peril to
affert, but upon fure and *unqueftionable* grounds.

Nor is the caufe of Chriftianity fo *immaterial* a point of enquiry, as you feem too fondly to imagine, and which has been fo frequently the fubject of debate between us. What ! fhall the Maker
of Heaven and earth be *faid* to addrefs his creatures in the language
of *men*, and they either treat *him*, through whom he fpeaks to them,
with open fcorn ; or carelefsly *unconcern* themfelves, whether he
fpeaks to them or not ? Shall an embaffador from temporal maje-
fty and power claim fo much, and one from Heaven fo little reverence and refpect ? If you doubt, do you think it neceffary to in-
quire into the credentials of the one, and will you not be at the fame
pains to examine the pretenfions of the other ? How does this
confift with the dictates of even common fenfe or common gratitude ? *You* may perhaps thank your God, with the proud Pharifee
in the Gofpel, that you are not as other men are, *extortioners, unjuft, adulterers, &c. you* may poffibly tranfcribe into outward practice that law within your breaft, to which we fuppofe revelation
comes in aid ! *you* may want none of its imagined motives to in-

　fluence

fluence your conduct—*you* may perhaps be able, unaffifted by any external guides, to learn, and live within, the meafures of your duty to God, your neighbour, and yourfelf; to do juftice, love mercy, and to walk, as you think, humbly with your God ; may contemplate thoroughly the nature and fitnefs of things, the native obligations and inducements to piety and virtue, and the inherent odioufnefs and deftructive qualities of vice and irreligion ; *you* may perhaps be inftructed from within yourfelf, in the knowledge of even the whole duty of man—Happy you, who *know* thefe things fo well! happier ftill if you *do* them !

But are there none in life who, with the *knowledge*, have not yet the *prudence* here fuppofed ? Or rather, are there not millions in the world that have *neither*? And fhall all your regards center in your own important felf? Have you no tender workings of humanity towards the wants and neceffities of your fellow-creatures ? Have you equally no regard for them who *know* not, and for them who *will* not *do* their duty? Have *you*, who enjoy the glorious light of the fun, no fenfe of the wretched ftate and condition of thofe who ftill fit in darknefs? What if *you*, through a whimfical contempt of day, fhould choofe rather to purfue the bufinefs of your ordinary calling in the night; muft day-light be therefore of lefs benefit and importance to the more rational part of the world? If *you* are whole and need not a phyfician, muft they that are fick not be prefcribed to ? I will grant *you*, for argument fake, to be poffeffed of right rational fentiments of the Deity, and to be verfed in every fpecies of worfhip and fervice that it is neceffary you fhould pay him.

But are you fure you are indebted to revelation for no part of this knowledge ? If that be the cafe, how comes it to pafs, that there are fo many inconfiftencies in thofe corners of the world,

where

where the rays of revelation have not been *permitted* yet to reach, in both thofe particulars ? How comes it, that thofe grofs abfurdities in the heathen worfhip of old, are in part continued among the pagan *Indians* (in the extenfive empire of the Great Mogul) to this Day ?—The darknefs, alas ! which thofe unhappily labour under, how furely is it owing to a perverfe, *uncontrouled*, inhuman exertion of power in thofe *rulers* over them, who unwarrantably intercept from them the important light.

But whilft kings of the earth ftand up, and rulers take counfel together, againft the religion of the Lord's anointed ; fome by diverting that ftream of divine benevolence, which means to flow alike to all, from its genuine and natural courfe; others, by polluting it with impious and unwholfome vanities ; let me wifh *you* to take care, that *you* do not ftand charged with the lamentable guilt of either, directly or indirectly, impeding its progrefs within *your* fphere of action.—Let me wifh that *you* would be as induftrious in inquiring into its real excellencies, as *you* are to expofe its imagined imperfections—Let not popular prejudice gain an afcendancy over reafon. On reafon Chriftianity is founded—Let reafon therefore be the judge (the only judge) to determine the merit of its pretenfions.

What regard the Heathens would have paid to a *divine* revelation, had they been favoured with one, may be gathered from their efteem of the Sybilline Oracles. For when thofe books were burnt with the temple, during the wars of Marius and Sylla, the lofs was deemed the greateft that could happen to the Roman republic, and people were fent into all the provinces of the empire, and to the neighbouring villages, ftreets, and alleys, to gather up what could be found of thofe books, and a collection was made, to apply to as before upon extraordinary occafions. And before thofe books were
known,

known, Numa Pompilius, to give a fanction to his laws, fpread a
report of his frequently converfing with the nymph Egeria, which
wonderfully difpofed the people to receive all his new regulations,
as fo many divine infpirations.   Hence it appears, that the Heathens faw the neceffity, believed the poffibility, and earneftly defired
the happinefs of a fupernatural inftructor and director.

But, alas ! to what fatisfactory purpofe, fay you, fhall a man engage in an enquiry of this kind, fo productive as it is, of never-
ending difputes ?   Why fhould I not content myfelf, with endeavouring to difcharge all the more *immediate* duties of morality, which
is in fact acting up to, or anfwering, as far as is incumbent on each
individual, all the ends and purpofes of revelation ?—A queftion,
which I will anfwer by *another*, alike pertinent—It is this—Can
any point of knowledge be of equal importance, with that which,
in any degree, refpects a man's falvation ?   And, if it is not impoffible (but on the contrary highly probable) that God may have
made, from time to time, fome exprefs, fome more explicit declarations of his *will*, can any thing be more unjuft, ungenerous, and un-
wife, not to enquire what that will is ? Is your happinefs dependent
on his pleafure, and will you not ufe your endeavours to learn what
his *whole* pleafure is ? Is it of no confequence to be informed how to
arrive to a right knowledge of the only true God and Saviour of
mankind ; that he will have mercy and not facrifice :—that he
delighteth not in the blood of bulls and of goats, or of men ?
(and yet had your education been among thofe with whom *religious* barbarities of the latter fort prevailed, are you fure you fhould not
have *confcientioufly* complied with them ?) that the facrifice of carnal
lufts and appetites, are the oblations he requires ? Is it of no moment
to be directed to the *means* proper for obtaining pardon and forgive-
nefs for paft offences ? Are there any meafures prefcribed by *natural*
religion for that purpofe? No. Whither then but to *revealed*, would
you

you go for methods proper to appeafe your offended God ? or does the *religion of reafon and nature* direct you to imagine you may be at liberty to offend, and he not authorifed to take vengeance on the offence, or remit the punifhment due to it, on what terms he him. felf fhall propofe ? But thofe terms, how fhall they be known but by revelation ?

True it is, he brought you into being by no voluntary con-current act or confent of your own ; but, if from that arbitrary exertion of creative power in the Deity, which gave birth to the frail creature you are, you lay claim to an exemption from future mifery, notwithftanding any tranfgreffions in life, you may have fallen into; I would afk you to whom you are indebted, for the *means* afforded you for obtaining *happinefs?* And with whom lies the blame, if future *mifery* is your portion ? He that made you ca-pable of finning, enabled you at the fame time, to fee not only into the natural and deftructive tendency of fin, but alfo into the advan-tages refulting from a life of virtue.

When two ways lie before me on my journey, I am doubtful perhaps in my choice, whether of the two to take. One, conver-fant in the country, fays to me, Go you here, and you are fure to meet with bogs or quickfands in your way ; go you there, and you will find a country fafe, fruitful, and delightfome. Whether of the two directions is it moft likely I fhall purfue ? The latter, moft affuredly—but that there are, I am told, fome favourite recre-ations in the way, peculiar to that other road, which I would willingly indulge myfelf in, though at the hazard of my life. Well, I go, and am loft. To what, let me afk, but my own way-ward mifconduct, can I with any propriety afcribe my mifcar-riage ? You will urge to me, perhaps, that however man's freedom of action may be illuftrated by the cafe here fuppofed, yet it does by

no

no means remove the difficulties more immediately under consideration. For as futurity is present to the Deity, all those lapses which may affect my *salvation*, must necessarily have been foreknown to him, ere my mother conceived me; how then does it confist with the suppofed goodnefs of that Being, to bring me into a state, which he knew *would* terminate in my entire ruin?

For a full difcuffion of this point of enquiry, I muft refer the reader to my Treatife on *Predeflination*, &c. while I pafs on to fome other remarks on our Deift, whom I left deducing from Mr. *Chandler's* declaration——" that if natural religion is not a part of the " religion of Chrift, 'tis fcarce worth while at all to enquire what " his religion is," (p. 6.) the following conclufion, *viz.* ' that then ' the other parts of the religion of Chrift, are fcarce worth any ' thing at all of our notice. So excellent and glorious a part of ' the Chriftian *inftitution*, fays he, is true deifm: and that, not- ' withftanding all the abfurdity of Dr. *Waterland's* affertion, what ' he has cited from thofe judicious divines, Dr. *Sherlock* and Mr. ' *Chandler, proves*, that deifm is all in the Chriftian *inftitution*, that ' can poffibly approve itfelf to the true genuine reafon of man.' Our author's dexterity, in thus creating patrons to the caufe of infidelity, from among *real* and diftinguifhed *advocates* for Chriftianity, is extraordinary enough; nor is his method of reafoning upon the point, lefs remarkable.

' After having faid, that every thing enjoined in the Gofpel to ' be believed as a rational doctrine, or profeffed as a natural duty ' relating to God, our neighbour, and ourfelves, is an eftablifhed ' part of deifm; the fingle queftion, fays he, between Chriftians ' and Deifts, is, whether the belief of natural doctrines, and the ' practice of natural duties, are all that is ftrictly neceffary, with ' regard to the divine approbation; and, confequently, human hap-
' pinefs,

' pinefs, both prefent and eternal.' (p. 7.)   And is this at laft the cafe ?   Is the battle between infidels and Chriftians to end, after all, in 'a friendly fhake of hands ?   If the fingle queftion between Chriftians and deifts, is whether the belief of *natural* doctrines, and the practice of *natural* duties, &c. are ftrictly neceffary to falvation, I here take upon me, in the name of the whole body of *rational* divines, to join iffue with the plaintiff, and to declare, that the belief of *natural* doctrines, and the practice of *natural* duties, are always looked upon by *them, as neceffary, with regard to the divine approbation.*

And when he fays, that this is a queftion or doubt which univerfally obtains among Chriftians, he advances what, from a number of our moft orthodox divines, I could prove to be not true. Nay, thofe *duties (viz.* the belief of *natural, &c.)* are, in fact, the very bafis on which *Chriftianity* ftands ; and the only difference between Chriftians and deifts is, that the former *do* practife, or recommend to the practice of mankind, thofe above-mentioned duties, and that the latter, in reality, do not.   *For,* as I before obferved, thofe doctrines are *natural* doctrines, and thofe duties *natural* duties, as well what appear to be *mediately* or *immediately* recommended by God, as what arife from the dictates of *natural reafon.*   So that deifts, by rejecting thofe doctrines and precepts which evidently make a part of, are contained in, or may reafonably be deduced from the Gofpel inftitution, do manifeftly oppofe (and it concerns them much, to give the argument its due weight) the religion they pretend to efpoufe ; *viz.* the belief of *natural doctrines,* and the practice of *natural duties*—in other words, the belief and practice of their boafted ultimatum of deifm, the *religion of reafon and nature.*

And when I acquiefce in the *conclufion* drawn from thofe fix refined propofitions, as well as the *propofitions* themfelves, the fum

and ſubſtance of which is, ' that thoſe duties only are neceſſary to
' be believed, and practiſed by us, the *reaſon* of which we perceive
' to be founded in *nature*, and the diſcharge of thoſe in the beſt
' manner we can, is intimately connected with our happineſs, and
' the approbation of him, whoſe favour is better than life ; and
' that then, if any thing elſe is enjoined as a duty in any, even in
' the Chriſtian inſtitution, it cannot be neceſſary to be obſerved, in
' order to eternal ſalvation,' (p. 8, 9.) what will follow from this
very fair and honeſt conceſſion, but that the *Chriſtian* only is the
man (where Chriſtianity I mean has been taught, and is eſtabliſhed)
of true genuine religion, and that the deiſt is not; for as the ſum
of all religion is the belief of *natural* doctrines, and the practice of
natural duties, and if thoſe become *ſuch*, which are either *mediately*
or *immediately* propoſed to us by God (p. 9.) how can the deiſt pretend to be *religious*, and reject at the ſame time that plan of ſalvation, which is formed from thoſe very principles ?

Having kept pace with our Deiſt, ſo far as his refined definition
of deiſm goes, and ſhewn, that before he proves *that* to be agreeable
to *the religion of reaſon and nature*, he muſt make it appear that the
idea of a *revealed* religion is an abſurdity, and Chriſtianity an im-
poſition, let us proceed to the examination of thoſe difficulties
with regard to Chriſtianity, which he ſays, lie out of the *reach of
our reaſon*, to determine of their truth or falſhood, and thoſe inſti-
tutions which are confeſſedly *no conſtituent parts* of religion (p. 12.)
And here, after a formal harangue upon the buſineſs of the underſtanding, and the end of our creation, and that great caution and
circumſpection which he profeſſes to have obſerved in his inquiry
after *truth*, or rather in his endeavours to rivet himſelf in *error*, he
tells us (p. 13,) " that though it is ſaid by ſome, that Chriſtianity
" is grounded on natural religion, and is an improvement of it; yet,
" after all that has been ſaid to exemplify it, or that has been of-
" fered

" fered in proof of it, I cannot poffibly conceive, fays he, how an
" entire and *perfeft* ftructure (which is the cafe of natural religion)
" can be only a *foundation* for a perfeft ftructure ; or how a *perfeft*
" religion can be *improved*; or what is effential to man, can be
" but of fmall importance to him, in comparifon of what is fu-
" peradded, and to which his underftanding is inadequate."

Though our Deift cannot conceive how a *perfeft* ftructure can
be a *foundation* for a perfeft ftructure, will it therefore follow, that
an *imperfeft* ftructure cannot become a *foundation* for a *perfeft* one ?
The *religion of reafon and nature*, I fuppofe *now* to call our attention not only to *natural duties*, ftrictly, or *abftractedly* called fuch,
but to fuch likewife as are really *revealed* ; that the *latter* therefore
may be added to the *former*, I hope you will allow poffible ; and
if fo, that *natural* religion was not the *perfeft* ftructure *without*
fuch addition as *with* it.   *Perfeftion* is a term purely relative, and
may therefore oft times become a comparative *imperfeftion*.   That
which directs a man to an obedience *now* required of him, is his
prefent *perfeft* rule of action ; but would it be alike entire and *perfeft*, fhould a more extenfive obedience be demanded of him ?
Would it not neceffarily *call* for fome *fuperadded* notices and inftructions, proportioned to the *fuperadded* duties ?   And may not
what was once *effentially* obligatory opon him as *meer man*, be of
fmall importance to him, when compared with that *fuperadded* fyftem of duties, prefcribed to him as a *Chriftian ?*   Yes moft affuredly.   For what fays the author of the Epiftle to the *Hebrews ?*
The law, fays he, *made nothing perfeft, but the coming in of a better
covenant did ; by which we draw nigh to God*.   Heb. vii. 19.

But, obferve with what folemn abfurdity our Deift again amufes
his readers, and impofes on their eafy credulity.

Having

Having ventured to tell us with an air, which we are to interpret into a *well grounded* confidence, that what he aſſerts is moſt infallibly *true*, and that his preſent ſentiments may very properly be " termed deiſm, as *that* imports the religion of things, and not of " unmeaning or many meaning words——of the heart, but not of " the book; it is not nominal, but real deiſm, ſays he, I now in- " tend; and by which I would fain be underſtood to mean that " religion which conſiſts of only ſuch doctrines and precepts, as " appear to have their *foundation in reaſon and* nature," (p. 13.) and then having attempted to ſhew, 'that *Chriſtianity* is not *that* kind of religion, he vouchſafes to tell us, that he is *coming* to the *point*, well knowing that he was then evidently the fartheſt from it, when he ſeemed *endeavouring* to be neareſt to it. And what after all *is* the *point ?* Why, I think, ſays he, " that the grand foundation of " the difference betwixt deiſts, and the religious of all other per- " ſuaſions, is, whether any doctrine or precept, that has not its " foundation apparently in reaſon and nature, can be of the eſſence " of religion, and with propriety be ſaid to be a religious doctrine " or precept." (p. 14.)

Among the religious of all denominations, the Chriſtian ſurely may be allowed to make *one.* I would then gladly know of our author what ſect or ſects of *Chriſtians* aſſert that doctrines and precepts, which have not their foundation apparently in reaſon and nature, are *religious* doctrines or precepts—teaching, at the ſame time, doctrines, that apparently have not their foundation in reaſon and nature? If he goes to the determination of ſome *councils and ſynods*, he may certainly find not a few. And yet, even *then*, he may be altogether as diſtant from the point in debate, as were their *infallible* deciſions, too frequently, from the *truth.* Search the *Scriptures*, and let me ſee him prove from *thence*, a ſanction to abſurdities, of that, or of any other kind, and I will not wonder at the deriſive treat-

ment,

ment they meet with from him. Till he can do that, he is fighting with a fhadow, and evidently reprobates rather from prejudice than princple the merits of the Gofpel of Chrift. But to proceed——

" The whole body of Chriftians, fays our author, may be rank-
" ed under the two following claffes, 1*ft*. Thofe who maintain
" that doctrines and practices which have no foundation in reafon
" or nature, may be of the effence of religion ; and 2*dly*. Thofe
" who maintain that doctrines and practices, which do not *appa-*
" *rently appear* (pray obferve his *expreffions*, for they are incom-
" parably *expreffive*) to be founded in nature and reafon, may yet,
" notwithftanding, be of the effence of religion.

That we may not, for want of *method*, confound our author's diftinct arraingment of Chriftian writers, and the feparate claffes in which he has placed them, we will bring each of them under a feparate diftinct examination ; for which purpofe it will be neceffary, in the firft place, to take a view of the *names* of thofe who make up the *firft* clafs of Chriftian writers.—And here, left you fhould too haftily *expect* to fee *that* compofed of *all*, or of even any of *fuch Chriftan writers, as had obtained the greateft reputation, both for found judgment and nervous reafoning* (p. 2.) I muft charge you, as you value the credit and reputation of our author, to be *fatis-fied* with the fingle, though fingular teftimony, of the all-fufficient *Zynglius*.—One *good* evidence to a reafonable man, is as fatisfactory as a thoufand—And he (the great *Zynglius*) is pleafed, it feems, to affirm, " that God may, *if he pleafes*, out of the vaft fovereignty
" of his will, command all that wickednefs, which he has forbid-
" den, and make it our duty ; and alfo forbid all that holinefs,
" which he has commanded, and make it fin to us (p. 15)."

The

The extraordinary nature of ſuch a kind of doctrine as this, it is juſt as neceſſary for me to controvert, as it was for our author to introduce it—and that is not all; unleſs he could prove, that in *it*, is comprehended the united ſenſe of the whole body of Chriſtian writers. And, if that in fact is the caſe, how comes he to have been ſo ſparing of *quotations* from them? I ſhould rather have expected that he would triumphantly have uſhered in a few *Engliſh divines*, of *ſound judgment and nervous reaſon*, to have kept his *Zynglius* company. But, that not being the caſe, all he has built on his *firſt* claſs of Chriſtian writers, riſes to a ſuperb building indeed—a *caſtle*, however, in the *air* only.—Let us ſee then, if he is more ſucceſsful in his *ſecond*.

" Thoſe Chriſtians of the ſecond claſs, he ſays, ſo far agree with
" the deiſts, as to own, that God, who is infinite in knowledge,
" and can never know things to be otherwiſe than they are in
" themſelves, cannot poſſibly conſider, nor conſtitute any doctrine
" or precept, to be of the eſſence of religion, which is not ſo in it-
" ſelf, as not being founded in truth and reaſon (p. 15.)."

An obſervation which (it being juſt expreſſive of common ſenſe) our author is pleaſed to make the *diſtinguiſhing* characteriſtic of the *ſecond* claſs of Chriſtian writers; and, what is more, to compliment it with the *deiſts* ſolemn ſanction, and yet, no ſooner are they thus happily and amicably joined together, than (moſt unfortunately) an officious *but*, ſets them at once aſunder.

" They agree, ſays our author, with the deiſts, in owning, that
" God, who is infinite in knowledge, and can never know things
" to be otherwiſe than they are in themſelves, cannot poſſibly con-
" ſider, nor conſtitute any doctrine or precept to be of the eſſence
" of religion, which is not ſo in itſelf. *But* then they agree, as
" the

" the religion of nature thus abfolutely confidered, and in its full
" extent, is only known to God, if he fhould be pleafed to make a
" *fupernatural* revelation of fuch parts of that law to us, which our
" *unaffifted* reafon could never have difcovered, *fuch* a revelation
" ought to be gratefully received, and readily acknowledged. And
" this, he tells us, we alledge to be the cafe of all fpeculative, me-
" taphyfical, and fublime doctrines contained in the Scriptures,
" which collectively compofe the Chriftian faith (p. 16.)."

And where, let me afk, lies the abfurdity in this cafe ? Our Deift grants, that God annot *poffibly* confider or conftitute any doctrine or precept to be of the effence of religion, which is not fo of
itfelf: what fhould hinder us then from acknowledging thofe things
to be of the very effence of religion, which we fuppofe him actually to have confidered, *conftituted, and appointed*—though they be
even fuch things as our *unaffifted reafon* could not have difcovered
to have been fo ? His firft conceffion fuppofes every thing *appointed* by God to be truly confiftent with religion, and confequently, that it is inconfiftent with *the religion of reafon and nature*, to
oppofe what he actually *has* appointed (p. 16.).

Ah ! but fays he, they *(i. e.* the rational Chriftians) go farther
ftill than all this : for *they* fay, " though no doctrine that has not
" its *foundation in reafon and nature*, can be truly a religious doc-
" trine, yet doctrines that have fuch a foundation (though that
" *does not appear)* may, if God pleafes, be communicated to us,
" either by himfelf immediately, or mediately by his agents, with-
" out any reflection on, or repugnancy to, any one of his attri-
" butes (p. 16.)."

The unfairnefs of this reprefentation of Chriftianity, is, I prefume, obvious enough to every one, who thinks not, or writes
not,

not, with the partiality of a deiſt. For all that men of any importance in the great buſineſs of explaining ſcripture truths,—in
other words, all that the *rational* divines have advanced on this
point, is, that it is no argument of *weak* credulity, or of an *irra-
tional* foundation for our faith, if, in the general plan of revelation,
there are ſome circumſtances *not* revealed, which lie beyond the
reach of our enquiries and that things in *this* reſpect may be, *in-
comprehenſible*, and yet not *incompatible* with reaſon, or the pur-
port of revelation. The errors and abſurdities which the patrons
of either popery or enthuſiaſm may have unwarrantably ingrafted
on Chriſtianity, and which have in reality no foundation in the
religion of reaſon and nature, affect not the real intrinſic merit of the
latter, and it muſt be ignorance, or downright knavery in a writer,
to lay them to the charge of the Chriſtian church.

Our *Deiſt* then having ſo very *juſtly* and *judiciouſly* ſtated the caſe in
difference, between *us* and deiſts ; obſerve the concluſion he *as* juſtly
and judiciouſly draws from it. " The difference, ſays he, betwixt
" rational Chriſtians and deiſts, will, without any farther trouble,
" be adjuſted, when this propoſition, which Chriſtians lay down
" for a certain truth," *viz.* " that the collections of writings, com-
" monly called the Scriptures, are of divine inſpiration, and a reve-
" lation from God to mankind;——be plainly and clearly made ap-
" pear to be ſo ; and therefore the material queſtion depends upon
" the proof that is to be made by Chriſtians, that the Scriptures are
" a divine revelation, and the very word of God. For if that point
" be proved, ſays he, the controverſy is at an end, there being no
" true deiſt that will heſitate a moment to allow, that what God
" ſaith, is truth (p. 16, 17, 18.)." Which is declaring, in as expreſs terms as can be imagined, that if Chriſtians can but once
prove to Deiſts, that the Scriptures are of divine original and authority, we deiſts will abſolutely acquieſce in all thoſe doctrines which

are *deduced* from them, even though they appear not to have their foundation in *the religion of reason and nature.*

Here then you see the ultimate resolution of a deist. If you will not suffer him to enjoy in peace the principles of a deist, he will, rather than become a *true* Christian, be content to be a Papist or enthusiast; for who but such as those pretend to ground the obligation of believing things not founded in *reason* and the *nature* of things, on any pretended authority from holy writ? —But passing by the compliment here paid by our author to Popery, enthusiasm, and superstition, let us attend him in his enquiry into the *asserted* authority of Scripture, which he promises to carry on with the utmost *impartiality.*

" Alas; alas! says he, here we have a surprising instance of
" the want of *unanimity* among Christians, where it seems to be
" so peculiarly requisite, that *without* it, they must not only
" expect to fail of convincing deists of the truth of their cause,
" but also render it a doubtful point, whether they are rationally
" convinced of the truth of it themselves. For if we begin with
" the Roman Catholicks, who have vastly the advantage in point
" of numbers, and plainly ask *them*, how know you the Scripture
" to be the word of God?—*They* answer, by the testimony of the
" church (p. 18.)."

Now I would venture to appeal to any man of common sense and understanding, whether the Popish method of proving the *sense* of Scripture, from the *implicit* testimony of *their church*, is of any weight in our author's arguments for disproving the *Scriptures to be the word of God.* Nay, he acknowledges, that the weakness and absurdity of this method of proof has been so fully shewn by some eminent *Protestants*, as to render it perfectly needless for deists to make any repetition of what is so generally known and

H

approved (p. 19.). What a trifler then, even from his own confession, is our worthy friend the Deist;—But now for the principal answers vouchsafed to us by *Protestants.*—" Why the one part, " says he, maintain, that they are known to be the word of God by " *themselves,* to those only whose eyes the spirit of God is pleased " in a distinguishing manner to open, to *perceive* the certain cha- " racters of divine truths in them (p. *ib.*). Another sort maintain, " that they are known, and will manifestly appear to be the word " of God by *themselves,* upon an honest investigation of mere na- " tural reason, to any man who shall impartially exercise it about " them (p. *ib.*)" meaning what follows from Mr. *Pemble.*

Mr. Pemble in his Treatise of Grace and Faith says " We know the Scriptures are the word of God by *themselves,* the Spirit of God opening our eyes to see those natural and lively characters of divine truth, which are imprinted on those sacred volumes. But how (asks he a little after) does the Holy Ghost reveal unto us the *truth* of Scripture? (He answers) by removing those impediments that hinder, and bestowing those *graces, illuminations,* and *sancti-fication,* that make us capable of the knowledge,* ——Bravo, my dear Deist!——and those whose eyes the Spirit of *God* does not open are—Who? Why those most certainly " in whom, " as the Apostle speaks, the God of this world hath blinded the " minds of them which believe not, lest the light of the glori- " ous Gospel of Christ, who is the image of God, should " shine unto them."

Well—The Roman *Catholicks* in *their* turn, continues our Deist, reply, that Scripture is delivered to most Protestants as by *transla-tions,* from men, who by their *contrary translations,* have proved themselves *fallible*; therefore granting that the *originals* be true,

* See our author, p. 19, 20. See also Dupin's Biblioth. Autor.

the

the *tranflations* may be far otherwife, at leaft, only one can be the true one, and which muft that be?

Why, that for which you have the beft and moft *reafonable* evidence—Becaufe " alterations in language, are, as our Deift " avers, unavoidable (p. 21.);" muft there therefore of courfe be no fuch thing as *true* language?—But fays he, in reply, " As " they might poffibly be corrupted by tranfcribers, and we can- " not be certain that they were not, the Scriptures, in thofe lat- " ter ages, cannot be proved to be the word of God, by *themfelves*. " For fhall we know them to be fo by their own teftimony con- " cerning themfelves, or by the reafonablenefs and apparent truth of " each and all the doctrines and precepts contained in them? " (p. 21.)"

If by the teftimony of Scripture concerning *themfelves*, our au- thor had meant nothing more than a teftimony arifing from the rea- fonablenefs of their doctrines and precepts, I would afk him, whe- ther the reafonablenefs of a doctrine is not one of the ftrongeft arguments, though not the only one, to be expected in fupport of its credibility?   " Well, but fays he, the affurance of the in- " fallibility and infpiration of the feveral *authors* of thofe books " called the Bible, is the very point in queftion, and requires to be " proved." Here again he fubjoins this very fhrewd remark (as if it had been a point of univerfal difpute among Chriftians) that its own teftimony, concerning itfelf, can be no proper evidence (p. 22.).

He is in too great a hurry to afk us, whether we have or have not any other proof of the infpiration of the *authors* of thofe books called the Bible, than what arifes from their *own* teftimony concern- ing themfelves, well knowing that we have many; for one of

which

which I muſt refer you to a note below,* leſt I ſhould loſe ſight of
our Deiſt in his haſty tranſition to the *ſecond* kind of proof of the
divine authority of the holy Scriptures, *viz.* the reaſonableneſs
and apparent truth of each of its doctrines and precepts reſpectively. " This, ſays he, is not ſo much as pretended by *thoſe* Pro-
" teſtants, whoſe anſwer we are now particularly conſidering."
Well, and how can we help it if it is not? Are the ſuppoſed abſurdities of one claſs of men to be placed to the account of the
whole body of Chriſtian writers?—As well may we aſſert, that
there is no ſuch thing in the world as right reaſon, becauſe our author, whilſt he pretends to eſpouſe it, ſhews ſo little of it in his
writings. But to proceed—

" *They (i. e.* Mr. *Pemble)* eſteem mere morality, and the bare ex-
" erciſe of our natural powers in matters of religion, altogether in-
" effectual with regard to ſalvation : things beyond morality, and
" out of the verge of human reaſon, they are ſo well aſſured are
" not to be acquired by reaſon, that they aſcribe the acquiſition of
" them wholly to the operation of the Holy Ghoſt (p. *ib.).*" Do
they ſo? and what then? Do *they (viz.* that body of Proteſtants
repreſented by Mr. *Pemble)* declare, that mere morality, or the bare

---

* Not to inſiſt upon other arguments, which might be alledged with great ſtrength
and cogency of reaſon; that complete ſyſtem of morals, which gives ſo great a luſtre
to their writings is, I think, a ſufficient proof that the Evangeliſts, and the reſt of
the ſacred penmen of the New Teſtament, were divinely inſpired ; 'tis true indeed,
there is ſcarce any one precept therein contained, but what may be met with in the
writings of the heathen philoſophers, but then they are ſo detached from one another,
and ſo deſtitute of a proper ſanction to enforce them, and are ſo defaced by a monſtrous
heap of abſurdities, which are delivered along with them, that they fall far ſhort of
that perfection which ought to be expected, to make them come home to men's purpoſes, and render them of general uſe. Whereas, in the Scriptures, all the doctrines are ſummed up in a plain and eaſy manner, and in a ſmall compaſs, free from
any embarraſs, and at the ſame time that they exhibit to us a full rule of duty to
God, our neighbour, and ourſelves, have all the authority that either reaſon or revelation can give to recommend them, and are enforced by ſuch proper ſanctions, as
muſt neceſſarily have a great weight upon every ſober and well diſpoſed mind.

                                                                    exerciſe

exercife of our natural powers in matters of religion, is altogether ineffectual, with regard to falvation?——Yes——and the affertion is juft implying nothing more or lefs than this—— *viz.* that mere morality, *i. e.* that kind of morality, falfely *called* fuch, which would exclude revelation from the religion of *reafon and nature,*—the morality in fact of *deifts,*—is and ever will be ineffectual to falvation. A truth to which every rational divine you can name me, will, I am perfuaded, moft cordially fubfcribe ; and not only this, but agree with Mr. *Chandler*, that " the religion of " Chrift muft be *underftood*, before it can, or ought to be believed, " and that it muft be proved to be a confiftent and rational reli- " gion, before a man can be under any obligation to receive it."

When therefore our author took upon him to affert, from the one example of Mr. *Pemble*, that this is not fo much as pretended by any eftablifhed body of divines (p. 23.), and that none but fuch as Mr. *Chandler* were fo rational as to maintain that opinion, he does not do juftice to the church of *England* clergy. If they declare that a man muft be *fupernaturally* illuminated, in order to perceive the characters of divine truth in the holy Scriptures, what more do they mean, than that a man muft cherifh in his breaft fomething fuperior to the too *natural* difpofitions and bias of an infidel ; fomething more than the fuggeftions of pride, prejudice, and partiality (which too ufually ufurp the fovereignty of right reafon) to judge rightly of the truth of revelation.

Nor is *Chillingworth,* as our author would infinuate, the only great man among the feveral patrons of Chriftianity, who cares to own that " natural *reafon* is the only true judge in thofe contro- " verfies, where the Scripture itfelf is the fubject of them " (p. 24.)."

Mr.

Mr. *Locke* fays, that without the evidence and ufe of reafon, men cannot be able to diftinguifh divine revelation from diabolical impoftures.*

Mr. *Hales,* fpeaking of the *laity* of the *fecond* century, obferves, " That one great caufe of error was, that the people, through floth and blind obedience, *examined* not the things that were taught, but like beafts of burthen, patiently couched down, and indifferently underwent whatever their fuperiors laid upon them.+"

Mr. *Bullock* fays, " If I cannot depend upon the plaineft dictates of reafon, how can I be affured that any doctrine is a revelation from God ? If I receive it without confulting my reafon, then for aught I know, it may be an impofture, and I am every way as liable to embrace an error as the truth."‡

Bifhop *Taylor* has well obferved, " 'tis reafon that is the judge, fathers, councils, tradition and Scripture the evidence.§"

Mr. *Chillingworth,* Archbifhops *Tillotfon* and *Sharp,* Bifhops *Burnet* and *Wilkins,* Dr. *Scott,* and indeed all our ableft divines agree, that we ought to make ufe of our reafon, in an enquiry into either the authenticity of a pretended revelation, or the doctrines which it teaches. You fee then, that by the united teftimony of men of the greateft reputation for *found learning, &c.* that reafon was never meant to be excluded from our enquiries into either the fubject matter or authority of revelation. Nor does it

---

* Vid. *Locke* on Human Underftanding, vol. II. chap. 18.

† Vid. *Hale*'s Tract of Schifm.

‡ Vid. *Bullock*'s Sermons, p. 19.

§ Lib. I. chap. 2.

appear

appear, that even what we call *supernatural* matters, or, what seems to us to come from Scripture as such, are incapable of being investigated by that criterion,——" for *supernatural* mat- " ters are what our author charges us with believing, upon Scrip- " ture authority (p. 24.)." I admit the charge, and let the Deist make from it what advantages he can.—" Why," says he, " mat- " ters *supernatural* are incapable of an examination by *natural* rea- " son, and therefore are incapable of being apparently reasonable, " or being *approved* of as such," by our reasoning faculties (p. *ib.*).

If mere confident assertions were equivalent to real argument, I know not who would merit more, as a writer, than our au- thor——Supernatural matters, says he, are incapable of an exami- nation by natural reason. But wherefore? Why must it necef- sarily be beyond the reach of natural reason, to make a discovery of truths which were once *supernatural*; *i. e.* beyond the concep- tion or invention of the original strength of reason?—Truths which *still* lie out of the reach of human conception, of which sort there are undoubtedly not a few, are, and will be *supernatural* till *revealed*. But will it therefore follow, that *when* discovered they become not objects of our *natural* reason and examination? What I was not *able* to discover of myself (and all men were once upon the same footing, with respect to some particular truths with which they were afterwards made acquainted) was surely a *supernatural* discovery to *me*, when made by another person; and cannot my reason, do you think, enable me to determine rightly concerning the truth, falshood, or probability, of that with which I was thus *supernaturally* made acquainted?

And our Deist, will he dare to say, that even *Chillingworth*, and our other rational divines, are gravelled, when they come to the

discussion

diſcuſſion of this, what he calls, *unmanageable* point; and at a loſs to prove that the Scriptures are known to be the word and revelation of God, upon an *honeſt* inveſtigation of mere natural reaſon? (p. 25.) And ſhall he, with a ſneer, talk of a thing ' being what ' it is, and *more* than it is at the ſame time? And of a man's hav-' ing the underſtanding of a man, and yet diſcerning what is out of ' the reach of *human* intellectual faculties to perceive (p. 2.)?' Why muſt the evidence of ſupernatural truths conſidered as above (and what other kind of *ſupernaturals* are there, but mere *contradictions* and *inconſiſtencies*, which our church abſolutely diſclaims?) why muſt the *evidence* of *ſupernatural* truths, really and in fact ſuch, be neceſſarily out of the reach of *human inveſtigation?*

But not to dwell any longer on the evidence ariſing from the *internal* characters of the divine pages, let us hear what our Deiſt would object to thoſe *external* ones, *prophecies* and *miracles*. Theſe, he thinks, " even when we have reckoned up all the pro-" phecies given by *Sybils*, *Jews*, or *Chriſtians*, or miracles at any " time wrought, fall vaſtly ſhort of affording the proof or *ſatiſ-*" *faction* to be *expected*. For *they* never, he ſays, can *prove*, that " the collection of tracts, commonly called the Bible, were written " by the perſons reſpectively whoſe names they bear; that the " Deity immediately dictated to, and impreſſed upon the mind of " each writer, the ſubject matter contained therein, effectually re-" ſtraining each one from mixing his own conceptions with what " had been thus dictated to him; and that theſe books have been " faithfully traſmitted from their original copies, down to us, " without any corruption, alteration, addition, or diminution; and " then if prophecies and miracles fall ſhort of proving theſe points, " which moſt certainly they do, *then conſequently* they fall equally " ſhort of proving the Scriptures to be a divine revelation, and the " very word of God (p. 26.)."

Obſerve

Obferve now with what *fyllogiftic fagacity* our Deift attempts to reafon away the authority of holy writ. Becaufe the divine *original* of the *fcriptures* cannot be proved by a medium, by which it was never intended it fhould be proved, therefore it is not capable of being proved at all. He fuppofes that miracles and prophecies given forth by Chriftians, Jews and Sybils, are *urged* to prove, in the firft place, that the Scriptures were written by the very perfons whofe names they bear ; and fecondly, that thofe perfons were infpired, and infallible in every word they wrote. Now if that be the cafe, he can furely produce fome prophecies given *forth* by Jews, Sybils, and Chriftians, and miracles fomewhere wrought, to which Chriftians refer, as what were exprefsly given or done for that very end. Till he does that, his charge is groundlefs, infignificant, and impertinent.

But if he means to fay, that prophecies actually *accomplifhed*, and miracles really known to be worked by thofe very perfons under whofe names the *Scriptures* are faid to be wrote, have, added to the intrinfic merit of the doctrines they enforce, a rational claim to our attention, he fuppofes the very fact. And if evidences fo confirmative of their *authenticity* ftamp not conviction in *his* breaft, we may reafonably conclude that *he* would not be convinced, though one *rofe from the dead* to atteft it. And though *miracles* and *prophecies* do fall fhort of proving that thefe books have been *faithfully tranfmitted* from their refpective original copies down to us, without any corruption, alteration, addition, or diminution, what is that to his purpofe, unlefs he can prove that they ever were *appealed* to for that *end ?* *Parts, learning,* and *integrity,* are the ufually fuppofed requifites for the difcovery and removal of any difficulties of this kind, to which the Scriptures in common with other writings may reafonably be prefumed to be fubject. And had our Deift poffeffed an equal fhare of the *latter,* with his perhaps juft pretenfions

I   to

to the *former* of thofe qualifications, he would not have funk thus low in the efteem of impartial men, as a reafoner on *revelation.*— But to proceed :—

Our Deift feems very fagac'oufly to imagine, that we muft firft prove that every *tittle* of the writings of the Old and New Teftament was penned by immediate infpiration,. and that the penmen deliver to us *nothing* but what was actually dictated to them by the Deity, ere we can pretend to recommend thofe books to the world, as an eftablifhed repofitory of *revelation.* But this, let me tell him, was neither intended nor neceffary.

The *infallible teftimony* which the feveral writers received, and did afterwards give to the truth of the particular facts they relate, is fufficient to give them credit as *authors*, with all impartial enquirers; even allowing them, at the fame time, the general fallibility of nature as men. In order to do juftice to revelation, we fhould be careful to diftinguifh rightly the *man* from the *minifter* of *revealed* truths, the hiftorian from the prophet; nor expect infpiration where infpiration is out of the queftion. Some things are propofed to us in Scripture, as neceffary objects of our *faith* ; fome more efpecially for proper guides to our moral *practice.* Of the firft fort, are thofe particulars which the prophets and apoftles received, by either an articulate found from Heaven, or by vifions and other fupernatural appearances, or by prophetic fuggef-tions of the divine fpirit; the truth of which they did—What, my dear reader ?—Why *either feal with their blood*, or confirm *by extraordinary miracles.* Nor will it be at all difficult to diftinguifh truths advanced upon the authority of *infpiration*, from thofe which are recommended to our notice as matters merely hiftorical.

The

The facred writers, by a more ferious and fincere enquiry into the real truth of things, added to the many *extraordinary* lights they from time to time received, furnifh out to us a more noble treafure of ufeful doctrines and maxims, than are to be drawn from the moft elaborate refearches of other men, the obfervance of which they enforce by the difcovery of many important truths *fupernatural*—truths not attainable *by natural reafon*, which, and which *alone*, were the objects of their infpiration. Out of the four Evangelifts, two of them were eye and ear witneffes of what they relate, *viz.* St. *Matthew* and St. *John.* Did they need *infpiration*, do you think, to make them write as honeft men? If fo, a man is a fool to believe one word of *Englifh, Greek,* or *Roman* hiftory! The two others wrote confeffedly by the directions and inftruction of St. *Peter* and St. *Paul;* and were equally capable of writing with hiftorical honefty and integrity, as the former. So that it is not fo neceffary for the credibility of Scripture ftory, as our author would infinuate, that the fubject-matter of it in general fhould be impreffed on the minds of each writer; and every thing therein penned, be the refult of actual immediate infpiration.

According to our prefent *tranflation* indeed, it is faid, *all Scripture is given by infpiration, and is profitable for doctrine,* &c. 2 Tim. chap. iii. v. 16. The pointing of the *original* as it ftands in, among others, Beza's Tranflation, proves however that Θεοπνευσος here is put in *appofition* only—Πᾶσα γραφὴ, Θεοπνευσος, ᚷ ὠφέλιμ℗. that καὶ, inftead of *et*, is to be rendered *etiam*, with ες underflood, the *tranflation* fhould run thus—All fcripture, given by infpiration, is *even* profitable for doctrine, &c. *

---

* For the incorrectnefs and unexactnefs of Scripture ftyle, and different readers, vide Dr. Brocklefby, p. 20. to 26.

The

The Apoſtle's meaning from which words is, that all Scripture given by inſpiration, *i. e.* every *prophetic part* of Scripture, every prophecy given, or declaration made by thoſe ſeveral inſpired teachers and prophets, is a memento to our rational and moral conduct; and, when conſidered with due attention, becomes profitable for doctrine, for reproof, for correction, &c.

But to return : " **Our** Deiſt cannot *conceive* how plain and *ob-* " *vious* truths can be revealed, in a miraculous and *ſupernatural* " manner *(ib.).*" And where, I would aſk, is it required of him that he ſhould ? What more is propoſed to our belief, than that ſome plain and *obvious* truths (truths which are the immediate object of even *natural* reaſon and religion) are in the ſacred writings enforced by ſome *other ſupernatural* doctrines, *i. e.* doctrines ſo *ſupernaturally* made known to us, that reaſon alone could not *naturally* have attained to the knowledge of them—Such as God's creating, with a view of hereafter judging the world by *Jeſus Chriſt,* his ſending that very divine perſon among us, who one day is to be our judge, to be firſt our teacher and inſtructor, that by his life and converſation he might approve himſelf a complete pattern of *virtue* and *holineſs* here, and by his death and reſurrection, give *aſſurance* that he came to open to us a way to perfect bliſs hereafter.

Are theſe, I would aſk, intelligible doctrines, or are they not ? And may they, or may they not be admitted into our creed, without offering any violence to our underſtanding ? Let me, for the preſent, ſuppoſe our Deiſt to anſwer in the affirmative, and to admit that they are worthy and valuable truths, deſerving our utmoſt veneration. But what then ? " It cannot appear to *me,* " ſays he, that they were therefore *miraculouſly* and *ſupernaturally* " revealed; becauſe, in the *firſt* place, they have not been *proved*

" to

" to be fo ; and, *fecondly*, becaufe they are to be difcovered to be
" what they are by the human underftanding, in the ordinary and
" natural ufe of its faculties (p. *ib.*)."

Here I muft lay before you another inftance of our Deift's great
talent for fophiftry and falfe reafoning, and his dexterity in fub-
ftituting fplendid nonfenfe in the room of real argument. In the
firft place, nothing is to be admitted in proof of revelation, but
what meets with our *Deift's* folemn fanction. Secondly, Things
cannot be difcovered to be what they *are*, by our underftanding,
and the ordinary and natural ufe of our faculties, if they were at
firft made known to the world in a *miraculous* and *fupernatural*
manner. His reafoning thus on this point, I impute to his con-
founding the *nature* of *revealed* truths, with the *manner* of their
being conveyed. He imagines that every truth muft be in fact,
fupernatural, *i. e.* not capable of being known to be what it is, by
the *natural* ufe of our reafoning faculties, even *when* difcovered,
provided it was made known in a *manner* fupernatural. He that
fees not into the fallacy of this deduction, muft be but little qualified to judge of the force of any argument at all.

But again.—" As to all the myfterious and unintelligible parts
" of Scripture, they are the fame, fays our Deift, as if they were
" not written, as to any good purpofe that can be ferved by them ;
" and to fuppofe that they give forth unintelligible inftructions
" and propofitions to his creatures, is to prove God, in fact, a
" mere *trifler*." If by myfterious, unintelligible propofitions, our
Deift means fuch things only whofe *manner* and *form* of exiftence
are unintelligible, do but only confider, how many myfteries there
are of that kind in the fyftem of natural religion ; and then judge,
whether any but fuch arrant triflers as *himfelf* will pretend to oppofe
them to the prejudice of revelation. Whether or no any *other* un-

I

intelligible

intelligible propofitions have the pretended fanction of revelation, I may perhaps enquire, as I go along with our Deift's anfwer to a reply to the *author of Chriftianity not founded on argument*; which feems principally to have been the occafion of this very extraordinary treatife. The reafon for it is very obvious. *That* being a book, on the credit of which the very life and foul of infidelity feemed principally to depend, it was neceffary that an anfwer fo apparently conclufive, fhould not pafs upon the world, without meeting fomewhere with an *attempt*, at leaft, towards a reply. But how difproportioned our Deift's abilities are to his *endeavours*, to overturn the found reafoning of Dr. *Benfon*, we fhall eafily fee by the few following obfervations, which I offer not in the leaft in defence or vindication of the latter (for he ftands in no need of any) but to expofe the grofs fophiftry of the former. The Doctor fpeaks truth, honefty, and integrity in every page, and flafhes unwilling conviction even in the face of our Deift, as appears from the various fubterfuges to which he is forced to have fuch frequent recourfe.

It having been afferted, that the rational divines prove all things, and hold faft that which is good, and that what is good in all cafes may readily be diftinguifhed from what is evil*, " the inference " which our fagacious author draws therefrom, is, that as in mere " matters of morality, only reafon can readily diftinguifh what is " morally good from what is morally evil,—fuch matters only " can, he fays, according to this way of arguing, be cafes of im- " portance, that is, with regard to the favour of God and eternal " falvation (p. 31.)" Here our Deift thinks he has drawn fuch a conclufion from his antagonift's mode of reafoning, as muft neceffarily bring him under difficulties infurmountable; and difable him from proving matters of *faith* to be matters of importance.

* Vid. Benfon's Reafonablefs of Chriftian Religion, p.

But

But I would aſk, whether it is not the united opinion of the whole body of rational divines, that morality is one principal end of Chriſtianity ?   And if ſo, muſt not the means conducive to that end, ſuch as are its articles of faith and poſitive precepts, be proportionably important too ? *(vide* ſupra p. 47.)   And can you, I would aſk, ſeparate with any manner of propriety a belief of truths revealed by the *immediate direction of God,* (and not *natural* objects, perhaps, of our notice) from the catalogue of *moral* duties ? But " how, ſays the Deiſt, does it appear, that the grand articles " of Chriſtianity, when they are now no more to be judged of by " human powers, than they were before to be found out by them, " are matters of importance ?   And how can things with propriety " be ſaid to be revealed to the human race, of which man has no fa- " culty of forming an adequate idea or judgment ? (p. 34.)"

What gave occaſion to this query, was, an inſinuation that without the Scripture, reaſon, or men's natural faculties, would never have found out many things that are revealed in the Bible.*   It may be true, that many things revealed to us in the Goſpel, could not have been *found* out by the unaſſiſted powers of human reaſon ; but as I obſerved before (p. 90.) no concluſion can be drawn from that conception, that now they *are* diſcovered, they become not objects of our examination.   Till that aſſertion can be diſproved, the wretched cavil merits only our contempt.   But then, ſays he, " to " talk of a revelation of things to man, in aid of reaſon, which " though eaſily underſtood, yet reaſon cannot diſcover any proper " uſe that can be made of them, is alike abſurd and contradictory. " But ſo abſurd and contradictory a declaration is this, ſays he, " that God will judge the world by Jeſus Chriſt.   This, ſays he, " does not appear to have any foundation in reaſon or nature ;

* Vid. Ben. p. 90, 91.

" nor

" nor is there any principle or premiſes from whence they may be
" drawn.   God will judge the world in righteouſneſs, and it is a
" matter of indifference to the creature by *whom.*   And as reaſon
" cannot make any improvement of this doctrine, how can it be
" ſaid, with either propriety or truth, that it was given in aid of it
" (p. 35.)."

Becauſe a deiſt can make no improvement of this doctrine, is it
therefore evident that nobody elſe can ? or that what he himſelf
may advance on that head, does actually proceed from the ſuggeſ-
tions of reaſon, and not rather from ſome principle which beſt ſuits
him, for the preſent, to ſubſtitute in its room ? Is it not ſome confirmed prejudice, ſome inveterate obſtinacy lying in the way *between*
reaſon and conviction, which hinders *him* from reaping that advantage from the declaration of God's judging the world, by Jeſus
Chriſt that he otherwiſe might ?

" Admitting it to be a truth, that God will judge the world by
" Jeſus Chriſt, of what more conſequence to the world in general,
" ſays he, is the knowledge of this truth, than that there being a
" burning mountain in the kingdom of *Naples,* is an advantage to
" the people of *England?* Then this is a juſt objection, ſays he,
" againſt the divinity of this doctrine, becauſe it is greatly impro-
" bable, that God ſhould ſpecially interpoſe to acquaint the world
" with this, or any other truth, the knowledge of which mankind
" would do altogether as well without (p. *ib.*)."

There cannot be required plainer proofs of the deſperate ſtate of
our Ceiſt's cauſe, than are the mean artifices to which he thinks it
neceſſary to have recourſe for its ſupport. Like a fox, well nigh
run down by his purſuers, and unable any longer to truſt to a fair
and open chace, he begins to practiſe at laſt all the little ſhifts and
doubles he can make, to protract, though but for a moment, the fate
he

he fees unhappily approaching. Had this circumftance of God's judging the world by *Jefus Chrift* been omitted, and nothing more had been obferved concerning the *diftribution* of rewards and *punifh-ments* in another ftate, than that fuch a ftate would one time or another commence—how natural would it have been for men to have enquired how it came to pafs, that revelation, the principal bufinefs and boafted merit of which is its making difcoveries not at-tainable folely by reafon, fhould yet leave us fo much in the dark, as is here fuppofed, in a matter of fuch great moment?

The time *when*, the manner *how*, and the perfon by *whom* this grand affair is at laft to be conducted, are circumftances of informa-tion, which every *right reafoner* would naturally have expected from revelation ; nor do I believe, that even the deifts would have been the laft to have complained of fuch deficiency.—And if fuch be their hardened infenfibility and ingratitude, as that inftead of its being a motive to their praife and thankfgiving, they make this fo material a difcovery an additional argument to fupport them in their prefumptuous infidelity—I judge them not—there is one that judg-eth—even that fame Jefus whom they defpife.

As for thofe twelve propofitions, which our Deift has introduced with fuch an air of folemnity and importance, it may be but juf-tice to him and to the reader, to tranfcribe them, that the latter may make what advantage from them he can (p. 37, 38, 39, 40.*.)

I own

---

* 1. That the firft caufe of all things is a being, not only of the moft boundlefs power, but alfo of the moft unlimited and perfect reafon or underftanding.

2. That in nature, there is the right and the wrong, of every cafe that can poffibly exift, or refult from the infinitely various pofitions and modifications of either fimple or complex ideas, propofitions, or things, at leaft, of all thofe cafes that right and wrong can poffibly be relative to.

3. It

I own, that I think eleven out of the twelve might have been spared, and that the *last* is the only one which affords matter for a serious attention. But this I leave to your confideration, whilst I haften to investigate *that* which our author feemed to intend as a corollary.

3. It may fairly be prefumed, that infinite reafon is alone capable of diftinguifhing unerringly, betwixt right and wrong, in all and every of that infinite variety of cafes that ever has, does, or can poffibly exift,

4. How far each individual of the human fpecies can, or may in reafon and equity be expected, to go in conformity to the immutable laws of rectitude in judgment and in practice, is probably only known to God; and as we cannot know, fo we ought not to prefume to determine concerning it.

5. How deficient foever we are in the knowledge of nature, of each others intellectual abilities and moral conduct, much more of the abftract nature and perfections of God; yet we are, in general, as certain as we are of the exiftence of fuch a being, that he is poffeffed of every poffible perfection, and will not in the leaft deviate in his conduct from perfect rectitude.

6. Therefore if God will require a perfection of God (if I may exprefs it thus) from his imperfect creatures, but in proportion to the perfection of their reafon; for to produce a rectitude of manners more perfect or conformable to truth than they have reafon or underftanding to direct them to, is impoffible.

7. To govern our conduct by our reafon is our duty, and is all God requires of us; and to neglect to regulate our conduct by our reafon, in that proportion which God has been pleafed to difpenfe it to us, is criminal, or blame-worthy.

8. As there is no individual of our fpecies, but what has been more or lefs guilty of deviating from the rule prefcribed him by his reafon, either the whole fpecies are unpardonably guilty before God, or elfe repentance and reformation are the means of reconciliation with him, and of reftoring us to his favour.

9. That repentance and reformation are the natural means of reconciling us to God, when we are confcious of our having offended him, is manifeft, from their being invariably recommended to us by our reafon on all fuch occafions, as the means proper for effecting it; for were the cafe otherwife, they could not be dictated by reafon, as a means to that end; becaufe had they not a natural tendency to anfwer the end, they would be unfit for our ufe, on account of their fignificancy; and to make ufe of infignificant means, is a prepofterous and unwarrantable conduct; and to fuppofe what is prepofterous and unwarrantable can be the dictate of reafon, is abfurd and a direct contradiction.

10. Therefore to repent of what, upon a cool review of our conduct, appears to be criminal, and to reform it, is a detail of our reafon, is what God the author of our being requires of us, in order for us to do on our parts what he knows to be neceffary to our happinefs.

11. If

lary to all the reft, which is this: " All other means, fays he, (be-
" fides reafon) for procuring happinefs, that either have, are, or
" may be deemed neceffary, and made ufe of as fuch, by Jews, Pa-
" gans, Chriftians, Mahometans, or others, are unnatural and
" foreign to the purpofe, and confequently are fuperfluous and
" downright fuperftition."

If our author will give me leave to except two out of the four
inftitutions, above mentioned, I will, from my foul, join iffue with
him at once—But can he fee no difference in point of importance,
between the Chriftian and Jewifh difpenfation, and the Heathen
and Mahometan rituals of religion ? A fet of words jumbled together into fuch a confufed inconfiftent mixture of ideas, can be
paralelled only by the celebrated *Bos, Fur, Sus, atque Sacerdos*, in
the mouth of every fchool-boy. But that the Deift might not be
thought to give the preference, among this medley of difpenfations, to that which we call the *Chriftian*, he tells you at once, that
the " fuppofed fatisfaction for fin, by Chrift's death, is a doctrine
" entirely repugnant to reafon, and as fuch, to be rejected with
" fcorn (p. 41.)."

Whether it is, or is not an abfurd doctrine, it is not my bufinefs
to enquire, till it can be made clear to me, that the *Scriptures* advance that, or any other doctrine, in the *abfurd* fenfe, he or fome
others, may happen to *fuppofe* they do. I only defire it to be confidered, that fo far are articles of religion, fuppofed by *our* church

---

11. If God requires and directs us by reafon and confcience, to perform what he
knows is neceffary to our happinefs, he will certainly do on his part what he
knows is neceffary to the end, *viz.* forgive us our fins, and re-inftate us in his favour. And *if* fo, then,

12. All other means that either have, are, or may be deemed neceffary, and
made ufe of as fuch, by Jews, Pagans, Chriftians, Mahometans, or others, are
unnatural and foreign to the purpofe ; and confequently are fuperfluous and downright fuperftition.

to

to be obligatory upon our *faith*, and no farther, than as they con-
ſiſt with the dictates of *right* reaſon ; and that therefore let this or
that particular doctrine be enjoined by a *Luther*, a *Calvin*, or a
Pemble, as eſſential to ſalvation ; let the tenets of a *Whitefield* or a
Weſley captivate the giddy minds of the vulgar, and draw them
into abſurdities *(ſuppoſing*, I ſay, *that* to be the caſe) Chriſtianity
never meant to eſtabliſh, muſt all or either of thoſe *ſuppoſed irre-*
concilables be made *reconcilable* with right reaſon, or *revelation* be
no more ? And muſt Chriſtianity itſelf be a cheat, becauſe perhaps
there are thoſe, among its ſeveral interpreters and expoſitors, who
would cheat men out of their *reaſon*, in order to palm upon them .
their own enthuſiaſtic *antichriſtian* extravaganza's, for ſound, genuine revelation-tenets ? The *Magna Charta* of a Chriſtian is the
Bible, with this *peculiar* circumſtance attending it, that *no power*
on earth can claim a *right* to add to or diminiſh from it. Here
then let God and the Scriptures be true, and every man, every
wrong-headed commentator a liar ; nor think we that becauſe
perhaps ſome doctrines, *unwarrantably* drawn from ſcripture, are in
reality *ſuperrational* and *ſupernatural,* that therefore *genuine, unſo-*
phiſticated Chriſtianity is neither rational or natural.

 " But how, ſays the Deiſt, can revelation be ſaid, or at leaſt
 "·proved, to be an aid to human reaſon, when ſo many various
 " and even contradictory *interpretations* are put on ſeveral great
 " and important paſſages in it ? And how does it appear that thoſe
 " who ſo much value themſelves upon their being poſſeſſed of this
 " glorious additional talent, have been ſo much *aided* in the right
 " uſe of their natural reaſon, and leſſening the perverſion and abuſe
 " of it, as might well be expected from the pompous repreſentation
 " and high character that has been given of it ? (p. 42, 43.)."

When we talk of *revelation* as an aid to *human reaſon,* we can only
mean that the one has made (as I have before obſerved) diſcoveries
which the other was inadequate to, in its *depraved* ſtate of nature ; and

I   that

that a collection of writings (containing such a revelation) may have been preserved to us for that purpose, I see no manner of reason to dispute; but that those writings should not in some degree share the fate of *others*, and like them be *capable* of being misinterpreted or misapplied by the ignorance, pride, and prejudice, inherent in the frame of some, or by the dishoneft and disingenuous perversion of parts in others, I can see no manner of reason to admit: or again that there is a greater obscurity in the *sacred* than is obfervable upon the whole, in what we call *profane* writers; but whilst there are those not only of different parts, capacities, skill in languages, but of different *sects* and *parties* also who, instead of *searching* the Scriptures for a discovery of what is *really* contained *in* them, hunt only for a support of preconceived prejudices *against* them, who can wonder " *if such are not aided in the right* " *use of their natural reason and the lessening the perversion of it,*" as our author thinks might be expected?

But then how comes it to pass, says the Deist, if Revelation " was intended in fact to restrain men from vice in general, and of " confequence those prejudices and partialities above-mentioned, " how comes it that such prejudices and prepossessions should yet " abound? And why if it was intended to aid men in the right " use of their natural reason, and lessening the perversion and " abuse of it, has it proved so manifestly insufficient for those " ends? (p. 47.)."

If a *guide* to men's actions must necessarily *govern* them too, there might perhaps be some weight in the objection; though that would lie equally strong against *reason*, the Deist's unerring guide— And in fact so long as we admit the free agency of mankind, no argument can be drawn to the prejudice of revelation from the perverse ufes it is put to. " But yet it is *said*, whoever takes a view
" of

" of the Chriſtian world, and beholds the abominable wickedneſs
" that has rode triumphant in it, as well in paſt as preſent times,
" and obſerves how the Chriſtian religion, and what is called the
" Chriſtian revelation, has been made a cover and a pretext to the
" moſt baſe and vile deſigns, will ſee the juſtneſs of this reflection,
" that if revelation came in aid of reaſon there very much needs
" another revelation to be given in aid of both. And though Chri-
" ſtians are apt to boaſt of the great benefit that has accrued to man-
" kind by the promulgation of the Chriſtian revelation; yet it is
" much to be queſtioned whether the poor *Americans* have not too
" much reaſon to conſider the coming of Chriſtians, and the Chri-
" ſtian religion among them, to have been the greateſt evil and curſe
" that ever befel them, and that not only on account of the mil-
" lions of people among them who have fallen a ſacrifice to Chri-
" ſtian piety and zeal, but on account of that perfidiouſneſs and
" baſeneſs, and that much greater degeneracy of action and affection
" that has taken place and prevailed among them ſince the intro-
" duction of Chriſtianity (p. 48.)."

As for the bad *methods* taken to eſtabliſh Chriſtianity in *America*,
or elſewhere, it is very ſufficient, I imagine, to obſerve upon that
ſubject, that *Chriſtianity* is no more anſwerable for *them,* than *right
reaſon* was for the practice among heathens of offering up their
ſons and their daughters unto devils; and conſequently that the
deiſt's reflections on this head are as foreign to his purpoſe, as
were thoſe practices to which he alludes.   There are, what even
Mr. *Chubb* allows, many bad things practiſed by *Chriſtians*, which
are not the *natural* produce of, and ſhould therefore not be placed
to the account of, the *general plan* of the Chriſtian cauſe.—But to
proceed now to ſome notable remarks of our *Deiſt*, on this truly
noble declaration, that " reaſon is the inſeparable as well as peculiar
glory of every intelligent being."

" Reaſon,

" Reafon, fays he, is the idol the Doctor choofes to bow down
" to." I much wifh the Deift had not offered incenfe to a much
worfe. Let us however hear what he has to fay upon that point. " If
" reafon, fays he, is the infeparable as well as peculiar glory of every
" intelligent being, then it muft be a fufficient guide to every intel-
" ligent being in all momentous affairs ;" and then, after fome of
the moft refined *nothingnefs* I ever read (p. 52.) he draws the following conclufions as deducible from the Doctor's account.   1ft,
" That reafon is the glory.   2dly, The infeparable glory ; and
" 3dly, The peculiar glory of every intelligent being." And how
glorioufly he reafons on thofe feparate degrees of glory conferred on
human reafon, our author's own words in his 53d and 54th pages,
which I chufe to fubmit to the reader's obfervation in a note below*,
whilft I pafs on to another remark on his antagonift fhew fufficiently.

" Reafon

---

* *Firft*, If reafon be the glory of an intelligent being, it is fo becaufe it is that
by which alone he is capable of juftly arranging his ideas, and perceiving their
agreement or difagreement, and thereby of diftinguifhing betwixt truth and fal-
fhood, good and evil, in all thofe things in which his duty and happinefs are concerned ; and confequently whatever knowledge is ufeful in thefe refpects, it is only
to be obtained by the due ufe of his reafon or underftanding. *Secondly*, If reafon
be a glory infeparable from an intelligent being, it could never, at any time,
by any means, much lefs by the tranfgreffion of any one individual of the
fpecies, have been feparated from the whole human race, without finking
the property of intelligence to the fpecies (which is not pretended) becaufe
while any one continues an intelligent being, he muft continue to be poffeffed of every property effential to intelligence ; and reafon being fo fpecifi-
cally effential to it (in that higher fenfe in which Dr. *Benfon* ufes the term intelligence) that a being void of reafon cannot with any propriety be denominated
intelligent : and therefore a being void of reafon, that is, void of a capacity of
ratiocination, which will enable him to perceive the connection or repugnance of
his own ideas, when under a proper arrangement, and to draw juft and natural
conclufions from their proper premifes ; fuch a being cannot be accountable
for the ufe or abufe of a faculty which he has not, nor will God expect the performance of duties proper to intelligent beings at fuch a one's hands. *Thirdly*, If reafon be the peculiar glory of every intelligent being, then it muft be the peculiar glory
of the firft principle of life and intelligence. And hence it evidently follows, that

if

" Reafon was not defigned, fays the Doctor, like our cloaths,
" to be put on and off at pleafure, but it was intended for conftant
" and perpetual ufe; and which we ought to make ufe of, not only
" in the affairs of this life, but much more in religious affairs, which
" are of the higheft importance. But alas! alas! fays our author,
" it is a certain, though melancholy truth, though reafon was not
" defigned, like our cloaths, to be put on and off at pleafure; yet
" that *fome* of our fanguine divines, like labourers in fummer,
" throw off their cloaths the better to perform the tafk affigned
" them; they caft off their reafon the better to reproach and *vilify*
" their innocent neighbours for not blindly fubmitting to their
" duties (p. 55.)."

Had the deifts in return but luckily put *on* their reafon in ex-
amining the grounds of revelation, they neither would have
minded nor merited thofe revilings.   And if this great champion in
the caufe of deifm, whilft he fo ftudioufly avoided fplitting on the
rock of enthufiafm and fuperftition, had not ftruck on the fands of
blafphemy and profanenefs, but fteered judicioufly between the two
extremes, *he* would have made a much fafer and more reputable
paffage through life. If others have deduced from Chriftianity
doctrines Chriftianity never meant to eftablifh, their weaknefs or
wickednefs be to themfelves.   But will that leffen *his* guilt in not
attending with proper deference to the declarations it *really* makes?
If God has thought fit to propofe to our faith a fyftem of truths
truly rational and interefting, becoming the Creator to eftablifh,
and his creatures to embrace and reverence (and be it an unqueftionable truth that he has not, or the deifts *unqueftionably* throw afide

___

if reafon be the peculiar glory of the Creator, then it muft be the peculiar glory
of the creature, in the refpective proportionate degree in which he poffeffed it; and
that nothing which he is or can be poffeffed of befides, can, abftractedly confidered, be equal, much lefs of fuperior glory to him.

their reafon in rejecting revelation) muft thofe important truths be overlooked, becaufe others perhaps have annexed to them abfurditics and inconfiftencies of their own *framing?* Muft the original dif- penfation be defpifed becaufe it has at times fuffered the abufes of prieftcraft and enthufiafm? And what if fome call it a promulga- tion of the law of nature, and others a fuperadded revelation? What if fometimes it is one and fometimes it is the other, which deifts, with a fneer, obferve to be the cafe? (p. 55.) What! does this, I would afk, make revelation not revelation? There is fomething in brutes that unaccountably determines and enables them to provide for the welfare of themfelves and their offspring.—Some call it inftinct, fome reafon, fome a divine impulfe. Sometimes it is one, and fome- times it is the other.—But what then? Shall we difpute a known fact? Deny that there is fomething equivalent to an *intelligent* principle in brutes, becaufe we want a name by which to diftinguifh it from the reafon of *man?*—The end, in fhort, propofed by an inftitution (not the *name* by which it is called, no nor the bad *ufes* to which it is put) will alone determine a rational man to approve or reject it. And as revelation was intended to promote the practice of true re- ligion, it matters not by what particular name you dignify or di- ftinguifh it. It is fufficient (in negative duty I mean) if you do not difown, difhonour, or deride it. But to return—

It has been afferted, " that the more the works of creation and " Providence are fearched into and underftood, the more they con- " firm the truth of the Chriftian religion, and add fuch fupports " and evidences as could hardly be expected or believed (p. 151.)" Our Deift's remark on this affertion is fo very difingenuous and difhoneft, that I fcarce can have patience to beftow any notice on it; and yet I know not how, totally, to pafs it over in filence.

" If, ſays he, the conſideration of the works of the creation muſt
" enable us to draw *ſuch* concluſions from them, as give a proper
" proof of the divinity of the doctrine of the *trinity*, the *hypoſtatic*
" union, and all ſuch other *ſupernatural* doctrines and precepts, as
" conſtitute the Chriſtian religion, properly ſo called, it can work
" wonders indeed; to which, ſays he, I may add the doctrine of
" *tranſubſtantiation*, the truth and divinity of which is as prove-
" able from the works of creation as the others. And if reaſon
" is ſufficient for theſe things, then what is it not ſufficient for ?
" (p. 58.)."

If the Deiſt had been ſo juſt to his antagoniſt as to have given
his words a fair introduction, and not disjoined them from the
main argument he was upon, the inference he has drawn from
them would have been too glaringly inconcluſive for the moſt haſty
reader not to take notice of it ; ſo that he very modeſtly waves
doing the one, the better to diſguiſe his cunning craftineſs in the
other.

" Dr. *Benſon* having previouſly obſerved, that thoſe profound
" ſearches into the cauſe of things, and the formation of the world,
" made by ſuch great men as Dr. *Clark*, Dr. *Derham*, and Mr.
" *Ray*, &c. had added ſtrength to the more common arguments
" brought in ſupport of religion, adds—that the more the works
" of creation and Providence are ſearched into and underſtood,
" the more they confirm the truth of the Chriſtian religion ; and
" add ſuch ſupports and evidences as could hardly be expected or
" believed. If ſo, ſays our author, they muſt neceſſarily prove
" the doctrine of the *trinity, hypoſtatic union, tranſubſtantiation*, or
" the like ; and if reaſon is ſufficient for theſe things, what is it
" not ſufficient for ?"

Why,

Why, it is not fufficient to make a man *honeft* who is *determined* to be a knave. Excufe the warmth of the reply, to which I am provoked by our author's fcandalous fubterfuge. The Doctor's defign, in the paffages quoted above, was, to fhew how learned men had fully anfwered objections and difficulties ftarted by unbelievers; " by leading them into arguments of a more abftract fpeculative " kind; fuch as the creation of the world, the eternal fitnefs of " things, moral differences of actions, moral obligations, and the " like, the former of which being more diftinctly explained and " expatiated on by the help of revelation, and the latter fhewn fo " entirely to coincide with the end of Chrift's coming, ferved, as " he very juftly apprehended, to furnifh out fuch additional fup- " ports for the truths of Chriftianity, as could hardly have been " imagined by men not attentive to fuch reflections." How our au- thor therefore can be juftified in his laboured *conclufion* from thefe paffages concerning the doctrine of the *trinity*, the *hypoftatic* union, or the like, I leave only to common fenfe and common *honefty* to determine.

In page 59, our author quotes as follows, from his antagonift. " As the Gofpel, fays the Doctor, (p. 233.) was a matter of pure " revelation, St. *Paul* was in the right of it not to mix his hu- " man learning with it; but faithfully to preach the Gofpel in " that purity and fimplicity in which he had received it from " Chrift. Our Deift's conclufion from thefe words is, that na- " tural philofophy or human learning cannot be exercifed about " it without corrupting and defiling it; and that therefore the " Doctor had gone beyond himfelf, and has carried the matter too " far (p. *ibid.*)."

Whether his antagonift or our Deift is guilty of the miftake of going beyond himfelf, and carrying the matter too far, I will appeal

to

to the judgment of the reader on what follows, which, though an altercation between the Deift and the Doctor merely perfonal, will be thought, I imagine, upon a perufal, not altogether unimportant as to the fubject matter of it. "If, fays our Deift, reafon is capa- "ble of drawing fuch conclufions from the works of creation "and Providence in favour of Chriftianity as aforefaid, then St. "*Paul,* not ufing it to anfwer that purpofe, muft render him not "commendable, but on the contrary greatly blameable. For when "he went from place to place preaching the Gofpel at *Theffalonica,.* "at *Berea,* and elfewhere, nothing could have been more proper; "nor was better adapted to anfwer the purpofe of his miniftry,. "*viz.* the working conviction and the converfion of his hearers, "than for him to have exemplified his human wifdom and fkill in "natural philofophy, by drawing thofe conclufions and thereby "producing thofe evidences from the works of creation and Pro- "vidence as proved the truth and divinity of what he exhibited "to his refpective evidences (p. 60, 61)."

If our author had not ftopt fhort in his quotation from his anta- gonift, he could have found no reafon for this objection; it being moft folidly obviated by the Doctor's own words immediately fub- joined. "As the Gofpel, fays the Doctor, was a matter of pure "revelation, St. *Paul* was in the right of it not to mix his human "learning with it, *&c. For,* when he could work miracles, and "enable others to work miracles, he had a much fhorter and more "effectual method of making converts and eftablifhing them in the "faith, than from any thing he had learned in the fchool of *Tarfus,* "or at the feet of *Gamaliel* in *Jerufalem.* In renouncing his *human* "learning, he did not renounce common fenfe. But human learn- "ing could be of no fervice to an Apoftle to make him mafter of "the Gofpel, or to enable him to work miracles, though it may "be of great fervice to *us* if it be made right ufe of (p. 234.)".

The

The Apoftles, fays Dr. *Benfon* again (p. 221.) " took quite
" another method to prove the truth of Chriftianity. They did
" indeed make their appeals to *men's* underftanding, but in a diffe-
" rent way from modern apologifts—being endued with readier and
" more decifive means of conviction, more fuitable to the apoftolic
" character, to the bulk of mankind, and to their own neceffary
" courfe of difpatch. They grounded Chriftianity upon facts,
" they wrought miracles before the faces of their hearers, in proof
" of a divine commiffion ; and then conferred upon the converts
" miraculous powers ; thefe were immediate appeals to men's
" fenfes, and what the loweft of the people could judge of, and
" reafon from." What is this but dealing with mankind fuitably
to their intelligent nature? (of which deifts affect to urge the
neceffity, p. 61.) What is this but making " an appeal to their
" underftanding, requiring their affent in a proper way, and bind-
" ing them with the cords of a man? (p. *ib.*)."

But again, Dr. *Benfon* fays (p. 27.) " Are not thefe moral vir-
" tues (which are the *principal* things in Chriftianity) the very
" things which all true philofophers have ever attempted to re-
" commend? Can any thing be more worthy of God, than giv-
" ing men fuch a revelation, when men had confeffedly corrupted
" themfelves, and that to fuch a degree, that not only reafon
" or the light of nature was altogether unlikely to reftore true
" piety, but even that light itfelf, as *Tully* exprefsly acknow-
" ledged, did no where appear." And then it being urged by
the author of Chriftianity, whom he was then anfwering, that
when Chriftianity appeared, it was an enquiring age, he anfwers
(p. 134.) " Suppofe we allow it, as we readily do? What then?
" What would he infer from that? The Gofpel fpread in that
" enquiring age, when, as he afferts, reafon was in the higheft
" requeft

" requeſt and reputation, and ſpread with moſt amazing ſwift-
" neſs."

Now comes the moſt bare-faced miſrepreſentation of a man's argument, that a writer can become capable of exhibiting. " The
" Doctor, ſays our Deiſt, has averred, that the Goſpel is a mat-
" ter of pure revelation, and alſo, that the principal things in
" Chriſtianity are the very things which all true philoſophy has
" ever attempted to recommend. Again he informs us, that the
" world was in that profound darkneſs, when Chriſtianity firſt
" made its appearance in it, that reaſon or the light of nature did
" no where appear; and yet he informs us, it every where
" ſhone forth in that remarkably happy age, with ſuch re-
" ſplendency and luſtre, that reaſon was in the higheſt re-
" queſt and reputation." Good God, ſays he, is ſuch confuſion
poſſible?

Such a heavy charge of confuſion and contradiction, ſo *confidently* brought by our author againſt Dr. *Benſon*, was, I doubt not,
implicitly admitted by every *Deiſtical* reader as, among others, one
demonſtrable proof of their *patron's* moſt profound penetration.

And yet what more or leſs does it amount to, than a freſh
diſplay of his uſual dexterity in the exerciſe of his profeſſion, as
a dealer in ſophiſtry and miſquotations, which he artfully gilds
over with a few gewgaw expreſſions, in order to dazzle the
eyes, whilſt he is playing upon and miſleading the *underſtanding* of his readers.—He cannot perceive how the Goſpel can
be a pure revelation, and yet contain things which every philoſopher has attempted to recommend?—Had it been ſaid, that
the Goſpel contains thoſe things *only*, which every philoſopher attempts

tempts to recommend, there might, perhaps, have been fome foundation for our author's critical diffatisfaction and feeming afto-nifhment.

But what if, befide thofe duties which Chriftians and philofo-phers *unite* in recommending, there are contained, in the *Gofpel*, *motives* to the *practice* of them, which neither did or could arife folely from the *religion of reafon and nature*. This and this only the Doctor fuppofes to be the cafe, and had the Deift viewed the *Doctor* in that fair, intelligible and rational fenfe, he might, in fome degree have faved his own reputation as a reafoner, whilft he is thus fruitlefsly endeavouring to pull down the *envied* merit of Dr. *Benfon*.

But hold, fay you,—your friend the Doctor is not to get cleared from the charge of abfurdity and confufion fo eafily as you imagine. For, fays our author, *he* informs us, that the world was in that profound ignorance, when Chriftianity firft made its appearance in it, that reafon or the light of nature did no where *appear*; and yet *he* informs us, that it every where fhone, *&c.* He! Who? What the Doctor? Why truly, no.—

But the Deift, finding that the Doctor could not become abfurd of himfelf, and without *his* affiftance very charitably helps him out with a few words of his own, fo artfully flided in, that eftimating *aright*, the *penetrating* powers of his *admirers*, and trufting *am-bidexter-like* to a judicious management of a fingle *article* only, he aims—alas, how unfuccefsfully! to *difarm* the Doctor in a trice.

If you refer to the Doctor in p. 134, you will find he is only arguing from *this* conceffion, which for argument fake he had a

mind

mind to allow the *author of Chriſtianity not founded*, &c. *viz.*
That when Chriſtianity firſt appeared, it was an enquiring age.
And what, ſays the Doctor, would *he* infer from that confeſ-
ſion? The Goſpel ſpread in that enquiring age, when, as *he* aſſerts, (who aſſerts? Does the Doctor aſſert it? Is *he* not evidently talking of the aſſertion of the author of Chriſtianity not
founded, &c.—Shameful!) reaſon was in the higheſt requeſt and
reputation, though he before had declared, it did no where appear.
Is ſuch a groundleſs *charge* of confuſion in an antagoniſt *poſſible!*
Is it poſſible, in ſhort, that a man can boaſt being actuated by
the *religion of reaſon and nature,* and be ſo ſhamefully deficient in moral *honeſty* in his writings? Or is it poſſible, that
you, my friend, ſhould ſacrifice your reaſon to an implicit faith
in ſo preſumptuous, ſo prevaricating a *dictator?* But to proceed—

In anſwer to an obſervation, that reaſon is of conſtant and
perpetual uſe in all things concerning Chriſtianity in particular,
our author aſks, " Where is the man that durſt, on the prin-
" ciples of pure reaſon, attempt to prove, ſo as to convince the
" underſtanding of another man, that an unoriginated, uncom-
" pounded, immaterial, and pure ſpirit, ſhould, *like* one of the de-
" rived, compounded, material, human ſpecies, have a ſon?"

And I in return aſk, where is the Chriſtian, &c. that believes or
would wiſh to promote ſuch a doctrine?—*viz.* that ſuch an unoriginated, *&c.* being, has a *ſon like,* or begotten *after the manner*
of one of the derived, compounded, material, human ſpecies? I
would gladly know from what corner of the world, from what ſy-
nod, or council, or eſtabliſhed creed, has our Deiſt picked up
that ſecret? Into what *Creed-monger's* cabinet council has *he* been
admitted?

But

But I will not enlarge on this point till I have confidered another charge brought againft the Doctor as a *trifler.* " When fome of " thofe doctrines that are peculiarly Chriftian were brought on the " carpet, and it became the Doctor's prefent bufinefs in his anfwer " to the author of Chriftianity not founded on argument, to fhew " or prove them to be all reafonable, he inftead of that only afks, " fays our author, are not all thefe things highly reafonable? and " there he ftops fhort of his excufe—he forbore to enlarge, for fear " he fhould feem tedious, which his not having done, proves that " his book is all wafte paper (p. 66.)."—fo that in order to avoid wafting pen, ink, and paper, you muft, it feems, trifle with your readers all you can—muft amufe them at all events, though it be even with words no ways *neceffary* to the purpofe.

The point upon which our author thinks the Doctor *ought* to have *enlarged,* he thinks not at all to his *purpofe;* but *becaufe* he has not fo done, all he has wrote on that head is wafte paper. This is a conclufion which our Deift had an eye to as of confe-quence, I prefume, to himfelf; well confidering that if talking not at all to the purpofe would preferve a book from the fcurvy fate of wafte paper, his own famous work would ftand as fair a chance for immortality as any book whatfoever. But the argument againft the Doctor is—that when he afked whether all the doctrines of revela-tion were not reafonable, he did not take upon him to prove to our *Deifts* that they *were* fo.

The internal evidences of the truth of Chriftianity are thefe, fays the Doctor (p. 21, 22.) *viz.* " *that both the doctrines and pre-* " *cepts* of Chriftianity (if we take the fcriptural account of them) " are highly wife and reafonable." Let our Deift, if he can, prove the contrary.

M

Not

Not to waſte, however, yours or my own time any longer on our author's *inconſiſtent* attempt to *do away* the *neceſſity,* the *importance,* the *glory* of the *Goſpel. diſpenſation*—ſophiſtry not ſolid reaſoning being his *fort*—I now take my leave of him, little or nothing more occurring in the ſubſequent pages of his Treatiſe, than a very laboured endeavour to prove, that if the " *Koran* is *falſe,* the *Goſpel of Chriſt* cannot be proved *true,* without ſubjecting the Deity to an impeachment of *partiality* towards his creatures inconſiſtent with our ideas of infinite rectitude*."

I cannot however cloſe this *Addreſs* to you, my dear Sir, without reminding you, in the firſt place, that the deriſive inſults with which the *Deiſts* treat the *Chriſtian diſpenſation,* are ſo many concurrent completions of that expreſs Scripture prophecy, viz. *that there ſhould be mockers in the laſt days :---denying the Lord Jeſus that bought them---*and *ſecondly,* that *they* will, as we may reaſonably conclude, ſhare the fate of thoſe of whom the Pſalmiſt ſpeaks--- *He that ſitteth in the Heavens ſhall laugh---the Lord ſhall have them in deriſion.*

* See from p. 80, to p. 90.

I am, Dear Sir,

Yours, &c.

F I N I S.

www.ingramcontent.com/pod-product-compliance
Lightning Source LLC
Chambersburg PA
CBHW021419090426
42742CB00009B/1187